Cambridge

The city of Cambridge received its royal charter in 1201, having already been home to Britons, Romans and Anglo-Saxons for many centuries. Cambridge University was founded soon afterwards and celebrated its octocentenary in 2009. This series explores the history and influence of Cambridge as a centre of science, learning, and discovery, its contributions to national and global politics and culture, and its inevitable controversies and scandals.

Eton and King's

M. R. James (1862–1936), best remembered today for his ghost stories, was Provost of King's College, Cambridge (1905–1918) and of Eton College (1918–1936). In these memoirs, he tells the story of the times he spent at the two prestigious institutions, providing a vibrant account of the people and experiences that characterised them. Beginning with his first impressions of Eton as a boy, he lends a unique insight into the school, moving on to recount with affection his scholarly and teaching careers in both these 'royal and religious foundations'. Ghosts and games, choirs and Christmases, and dramas and dons are all recalled in vivid detail, creating a colourful picture of academic life during the early twentieth century and the First World War. Anecdotal, touching and often humorous, James' recollections reveal his role in both intellectual and social life at these famous institutions, and his dedication and allegiance to them.

T0370737

Cambridge University Press has long been a pioneer in the reissuing of out-of-print titles from its own backlist, producing digital reprints of books that are still sought after by scholars and students but could not be reprinted economically using traditional technology. The Cambridge Library Collection extends this activity to a wider range of books which are still of importance to researchers and professionals, either for the source material they contain, or as landmarks in the history of their academic discipline.

Drawing from the world-renowned collections in the Cambridge University Library, and guided by the advice of experts in each subject area, Cambridge University Press is using state-of-the-art scanning machines in its own Printing House to capture the content of each book selected for inclusion. The files are processed to give a consistently clear, crisp image, and the books finished to the high quality standard for which the Press is recognised around the world. The latest print-on-demand technology ensures that the books will remain available indefinitely, and that orders for single or multiple copies can quickly be supplied.

The Cambridge Library Collection will bring back to life books of enduring scholarly value (including out-of-copyright works originally issued by other publishers) across a wide range of disciplines in the humanities and social sciences and in science and technology.

Eton and King's

Recollections, Mostly Trivial, 1875–1925

M.R. James

CAMBRIDGE
UNIVERSITY PRESS

CAMBRIDGE UNIVERSITY PRESS

Cambridge, New York, Melbourne, Madrid, Cape Town,
Singapore, São Paolo, Delhi, Tokyo, Mexico City

Published in the United States of America by Cambridge University Press, New York

www.cambridge.org
Information on this title: www.cambridge.org/9781108030533

© in this compilation Cambridge University Press 2011

This edition first published 1926
This digitally printed version 2011

ISBN 978-1-108-03053-3 Paperback

ETON AND KING'S

M. R. JAMES

(By a Present Etonian).

ETON AND KING'S

Recollections, Mostly Trivial

1875–1925

BY

M. R. JAMES

PROVOST OF ETON
SOMETIME PROVOST OF KING'S

LONDON
WILLIAMS & NORGATE, LTD.
14 HENRIETTA STREET, COVENT GARDEN, W.C. 2
1926

Printed in Great Britain

TO

THE FRIENDS

WHOSE NAMES APPEAR

AND DO NOT APPEAR

IN THESE PAGES

CONTENTS

PAGE

I. FIRST SIGHT OF ETON. EXAMINATION FOR
COLLEGE I

II. TEMPLE GROVE. AMENITIES. MUSIC AND LITERA-
TURE. WATERFIELD. MR. PRIOR. GAMES.
HOBBIES 5

III. ADMITTED K.S. THE *Personnel* OF COLLEGE.
FAGGING. PURSUITS AND PASTIMES: THE
WALL, CRICKET, DICKENS 15

IV. SCHOOL AND COLLEGE LIBRARIES. MUSIC:
CHANTS, HYMNS, ANTHEMS. LAY CLERKS.
ST. GEORGE'S. MICHAEL WISE . . . 23

V. DIVISION MASTERS: WALTER DURNFORD, AUSTEN
LEIGH, WARRE. EXTRAS. MATHEMATICS.
SCIENCE. STUDIES OUT OF SCHOOL: HOW ONE
OF THEM WAS SCOTCHED 32

VI. THE HEAD MASTER'S DIVISION: ROUTINE AND ITS
DIVERSIONS. THE PRÆPOSTORSHIP. EVENING
CONVERSATIONS. LOCAL MYTHOLOGY. SIXTH
FORM SUPPER. NIGHT THOUGHTS . . 43

VII. SCHOOL SOCIETIES: LITERARY, POP, SHAKE-
SPEARE. THE NEWCASTLE. FRANCE . . 55

VIII. CONTEMPORARIES FROM THE BOY'S POINT OF
VIEW: TATHAM, CUST, FITTON. THE RIVER.
THE CORPS. ROOFS. SKATING. WOES.
NOURISHMENT 64

PAGE

IX. THE PROVOST AND FELLOWS. RITUAL OF CHAPEL.
CONFIRMATION. SERMONS : OLD JOYNES.
THE WINDOWS, EXTANT AND LOST. THE WALL
PAINTINGS. THE IMAGES. THE OLD REREDOS.
Contretemps IN CHAPEL. THE BELLS. THE
CUPOLAS 79

X. LITERARY ASPIRATIONS : *The Chronicle* : MY CO-
EDITOR. END OF ETON LIFE FOR ME : BE-
GINNING OF IT FOR OTHERS . . . 95

XI. KING'S. THE OLD SOCIETY. THE " SCHOLAR'S
BOOK." OLD AND NEW STATUTES . . 99

XII. PROVOST AND SENIORS. OKES, ANDREW LONG,
BRADSHAW, FRED WHITTING, AUGUSTUS LEIGH,
O.B., NIXON, CHURTON, WILLY LEIGH, COBBOLD,
MOZLEY. THE LATER DON 106

XIII. THE UNDERGRADUATES. THE TUTORS. WORK. THE
CAMBRIDGE DAY 137

XIV. THE DRAMA, CLASSICAL AND MODERN. GREECE.
FRANCE : THE BICYCLE TOUR . . . 147

XV. MRS. SMITH. TRADITIONS OF THE DARK PAST :
OUR GHOST 155

XVI. FRIENDS : HUGESSEN, MAXSE, BOYLE, MARCUS
DIMSDALE, J.K.S., WALTER HEADLAM, LIONEL
FORD 160

XVII. J. AND OTHER GREAT FIGURES : CAYLEY, STOKES,
MAYOR, KENNEDY. THE HEADS . . . 176

XVIII. A HOLIDAY AND SOME LYRICS. CYPRUS . . 189

XIX. RESEARCH. APOCRYPHA. MANUSCRIPTS. FOREIGN
SCHOLARS. THE BRENT ELEIGH BOOKS. DR.
JESSOPP. PROFESSOR KNAPP. THE LADY
CHAPEL AT ELY 195

PAGE

XX. J. H. MIDDLETON. ROBERTSON SMITH. ALDIS
WRIGHT. HENRY JACKSON. SIDGWICK.
JAMES WARD 209

XXI. J. MCBRYDE. WILL STONE. EUSTACE TALBOT.
MARK SYKES. HAROLD LUBBOCK . . . 218

XXII. OFFICIAL EMPLOYMENTS. KING'S CHAPEL :
WORK ON THE WINDOWS, THE EASTERN BAY,
THE HALL. THE CHOIR : THE ORGANIST, A
CHORISTERSHIP TRIAL. THE CHOIR SCHOOL
MATCH. MY DRAMATIC WORKS. A PRE-WAR
CHRISTMAS AT KING'S 226

XXIII. THE UNION. THE PITT. THE CHITCHAT (THE
APOSTLES). THE T.A.F. THE FAMILY : DAY
AND PRIOR 241

XXIV. THE FITZWILLIAM. MR. COWMAN. APOLOGY
FOR THINGS AND PERSONS OMITTED . . 250

XXV. THE PROVOSTSHIP. COLLEGE MEETINGS, KING'S
AND ETON. SIR HENRY ROSCOE. THE PUBLIC
RECORDS COMMISSION : DR. HENRY OWEN.
THOUGHTS OF A UNIVERSITY DELEGATE . . 254

XXVI. THE VICE-CHANCELLORSHIP. THE WAR . . 261

XXVII. RECALLED TO ETON. ETON'S LOSSES : ITS NEW
GROWTHS : ITS BOYS 265

XXVIII. EPILOGUE 270

PROLOGUE

IT was at the request of the well-known Firm who issue this volume that I procured a pencil and some paper and sat down one day last August to write my reminiscences of Eton and King's. I do not make this statement in order to turn away the wrath of critics or readers who may dislike the book, for it is not the request but the consent to the request that must bear the blame. Only I will say that I had never thought myself likely to write such things. I postponed the attempt to do so for a long time, and found it very difficult to make a beginning. Then— I suppose it is the oldest of stories—when the pencil had begun to run along the lines, the doubt was whether I should ever be able to stop it. Doors opened in obscure parts of the brain, and people and scenes and dialogues, many more than I supposed I kept there, peeped out and insisted on being marked down.

It was all a matter of remembering. True, I had old letters, and I had a note-book in which I put down very shortly the skeleton of each year's events, and more carefully the places I had been to in holidays, but there has been no Diary kept.

Nevertheless I believe it will be difficult to convict me of grave inaccuracy.

One or two strictures I will anticipate. In the first hundred or so pages of my manuscript the word " I " occurs on an average four times on the page : probably that average is kept up throughout. It is too bad. But the choice has been between periphrasis and direct statement, and I have deliberately preferred the latter.

I have made excellent people figure in a ridiculous light. Quite true, especially when I have been looking at them through the eyes of the boy or the undergraduate : but I have not often used a pen that had gall in it.

I have omitted or slurred over rows and unpleasantnesses ; the resultant picture is too smooth and bright to be true. Well, there were some I could have described, but not many, and what there were would have made poor reading. The general impression I give I assert to be correct.

My other sins of omission I have to some extent acknowledged in the text. Nobody knows better than I how many they are.

I have allowed too many trivialities and esoteric jokes to creep in. That is probably so : but who is an entirely fair judge of the quality of the jokes that amused him when he was a boy ? It is here that the reminiscencer is bound to give himself away most freely. Whether he ought to do so or not, he does write with an eye on the old friends to whom the jokes made their first appeal. To the reader who simply says " We are not amused " there is no possible answer. One can only hope for the best. The case of the trivialities is much the same. They are recorded because to the recorder they have seemed to give life and truthfulness to the picture. The whole book may be described as a study of still life ; in such a work the interest depends very largely on small detail. Again I say, nobody knows better than I how weak is the defence I can put up, if I am taxed with foolish, nay, senile, garrulity.

In several places in the book I have touched on my purpose in telling of this or that. The ruling motive throughout has been to show cause for the gratitude which I feel for the two great foundations of King Henry the Sixth,

ETON AND KING'S

ETON AND KING'S

I

ETON has a very large literature, and much of it is so recent that, in adding to it, one runs a great risk of telling the same story in different words that has been told by the Vice-Provost[1] and by Mr. Eric Parker.[2] King's also has had its illustrator of late in E. F. Benson—see his *David of King's* and *Our Family Affairs*—and its chronicler some years back in William Austen Leigh—see his memoir of his brother, the Provost.

Still, I suppose there is room to view both places from one's own angle, and to infuse into the survey some little doses of history which the standard authorities have not used up, as well as something of University doings and one's own various literary pursuits and investigations. Something like a true picture may be the result —but will it be interesting ? We can but try.

It was in July 1875 that I first set eyes on Eton, as a candidate for a scholarship. With two or three other boys I was brought from Temple

---

[1] H. Macnaghten, *Fifty Years of Eton in Prose and Verse*, 1924.
[2] Eric Parker, *Playing Fields*, 1922, etc.

Grove, East Sheen, by the tremendous O. C. Waterfield—whom Arthur Benson has well described in *Memories and Friends*—and lodged at the Christopher.

It seems odd, but, though my father was an Etonian (from 1830 to 1842) and I was familiar with many stories of the place, I had no kind of idea where Eton was, didn't know that it was next door to Windsor Castle, had never taken in the existence of Chapel, School Yard, and the rest. Yet, though I was amazed and impressed, I cannot pretend that I was at once spellbound, or vowed that it should be Eton for me or nothing.

Two things there were which embittered the days of examination, neither of them at all likely to be undergone by candidates now. One was the mob of large Lower Boys who lay in wait for us when we came out of Upper School or Lower School and made unfeeling remarks ; kicks too were exchanged. The other was Waterfield's appalling habit of making us bring out and show him the rough copies of our compositions ; a dreadful explosion took place at breakfast, when it appeared that I had put the subject of the sentence into the ablative absolute. Language comparable to that which the Doctor lavished on Arthur Pendennis rises to my recollection. " A boy who construes δε *and* instead of δε *but* at sixteen years of age, is guilty not merely of folly, and ignorance, and dulness inconceivable, but of crime, of deadly crime, of filial ingratitude, which I tremble to contemplate," *et reliqua*. It was bad policy, for it unnerved one for further efforts. I did get on the list for College that year, but the vacancies were few—only about half a dozen—and I had to try again, in July of 1876. This time Mr. Edgar, the second in command at Temple Grove, took us to Eton, and the atmosphere was calmer. No rough copies were demanded, and there was but little hardship in being taught how to do a simultaneous equation on the eve of the second Mathematical paper : though nobody must ask me what the process is now. All went well, and my name was second on the list.

Looking back, it seems that one was oddly incurious about the whole business. The examiners—Provost Goodford, in cassock, preacher's gown and bands, and old Sir Edward Creasy, author of the *Fifteen Decisive Battles* and much else—I do recollect, and (Sir) Philip Gregory, who kindly allowed me to pass in mathematics : he was then a Fellow of King's. But I don't remember thinking that it would make any great difference to my happiness whether I went to Eton or to Charterhouse (which I believe was next on my programme, and which I then imagined to be a Bluecoat School), nor did my contemporaries at Temple Grove seem to dwell much upon the excellences of the various public schools which *they* were going to patronize. The only partisanship of that sort which stirred us then was that which arose over the University Boat Race, which, of course, was rowed very near our school. Then everybody was Oxford or Cambridge, masters included, and we were far more interested in the result than ever I was when I lived among the actors in the contest. Otherwise we were altogether self-centred, as I believe little boys usually are.

II

WILL a page or two about Temple Grove be allowed, I wonder ? Arthur Benson has drawn a good picture of it in the book I mentioned just now, and E. F. Benson another in the early chapters of *David Blaize;* but I feel that I, too, owe it a tribute. It had the reputation of being the oldest private school in England ; could be traced back to 1792, when a certain Dr. Pinckney had it. My father went there in 1828 at the age of six, and we believed that Henry Bradshaw and Munro the Latinist had been members of it. To these names tradition—quite baseless—added Disraeli. Waterfield had been in command for some years when I went there, but I believe he did not actually own the place. The descendants of Pinckney were still landlords, we were told. According to present ideas it was too large for a private school—the numbers in my time were round about 130. So it was an alarmingly big community for a small boy to be pitchforked into, and the rainy day in September 1873 on which my father left me there is one of the most lachrymose in my remembrance. Farrar's *St. Winifred's* had served to form my expectations of school life, a book which, undeniably maudlin, is also undeniably absorbing. The characters in it I tried, of course, to find at Temple Grove ; and one or two seemed to fit pretty well. Arthur Benson, I recall, corresponded to Power, and Hubert Brinton to the humorist Henderson—but the book is no longer a classic, and I must not assume knowledge of it on the part of my readers. Nor do I mean to inflict on them a chronicle of the three immense years of private school life. The amenities were not many. If you were first or second in your Class in the monthly examination, you were put on the Honour list or " Honoris," a red cross was prefixed to your name on the school list (a blue cross for Mathematics, but I never was up to *that*), and you were allowed to go " round the grounds," a realm of shrubbery and groves beyond the playing fields, and on half-holidays you might go with a friend to Richmond and expend sixpence if you were not in the First Class, and, if you were, any money you might own. Somewhere on the road to Richmond, perhaps, has been found a silver coin of Vonones II, King of Parthia, which was given me by an uncle and dropped, with other treasures in a small carved box, on one of these expeditions. The banana, then a rather uncommon viand, the prickly pear, the Maid of Honour (of which I do not tire), and a horrid object called a tea-suck (being a sugar-stick through which you absorbed your tea when you got back)—these were proper things to buy :

and, more out of deference to Waterfield than because we thought greatly of it, black-jack, which was made and sold at a very small shop and was a rod of toffee enwrapped spirally in newspaper. This Waterfield believed to be our chief delight, and in moments of condescension would inquire if we had been making ourselves ill with it, and the like. But I do not think the First Class considered it up to their mark.

Now let us speak of higher things : Literature and the Fine Arts. Arthur Sullivan had been music master at Temple Grove shortly before my day, and I remember his coming on one occasion to hear me (and perhaps others who constituted the choir) sing. The efforts of the choir were confined to practising some few part-songs on a Saturday evening, after which they had cake and a curious kind of pineapple jam. " I sat beneath the abeles old " (what, we wondered, were abeles ?) " The meads were shot with green and gold, And underneath my feet there rolled The little silv'ry Gad." This, by an unknown composer, comes back to me, and so does Rossini's " Strength of the holy, virtue divine," etc., as performed by self and a nice boy called Goldschmidt, whose mother was—Jenny Lind. One day she came to see him, and he presented me to her as his friend.

But there was no such thing as a school concert, or any public exhibition of our talents.

Literature : what books solaced me most ?

The week-day school library afforded Curzon's *Visits to Monasteries in the Levant*, which I believe first inspired me with a curiosity about manuscripts : it had also a book of Spanish fairy tales called *Patranas*, which I have never seen since : like the ruck of ungrateful boys I probably never looked to see who wrote it for my delight. *The Water Babies* I first saw there, too. I don't doubt Scott was present, but I did not trouble him. Dickens and Thackeray I presume were not. Of the Sunday library I remember best Neale's *Tales from Church History*, particularly *The Quay of the Dioscuri*, a really entrancing story, Kingsley's *Hermits*, and above all the two volumes of *Good Words for the Young* which contained George Macdonald's *At the Back of the North Wind*, Gilbert's *King George's Middy*, and school stories by Ascott R. Hope. Two other week-day books, full of riddles to me, but extraordinarily fascinating, were Henry Kingsley's *Boy in Grey* and, what I daresay will seem oddest of all, *The Shaving of Shagpat*.

R. M. Ballantyne was the boys' writer who turned out his annual Christmas volume for our generation. The ingredients were capable of being tabulated. A comic Irishman, a dear old lady, an irascible old gentleman, an adventurous boy (sometimes a charming girl), a skilled hunter (or engine-driver, or fireman, or sailor). One chapter dealt with the history of the fire brigade, or the post-office, or the railway, or the lighthouse,

and the pages of this had less sardine oil and tea
on them than their neighbours. But everybody
liked Ballantyne, and he was much in request
from owners. If Orlebar *mi.* is still alive, and
if this page meets his eye, I would have him know
that I have not forgotten, and doubt if I have
forgiven, his losing my copy of *The Norsemen in
the West*.

Now here is a literary problem. There were
in circulation among us certain large quarto
paper books with full-page woodcuts which told
the story—in numberless episodes—of Prince
Pippin (and Princess Pansy) and his slaying of
giants, witches, sphinxes, dragons, and what not.
They seemed to me the last word in delight-
fulness ; but I never saw or heard more of them
until—I think just before the War—they began
to reappear in a much smaller size on railway
book-stalls. I bought all I could find and wrote
to the publisher for a complete set, but already
the early numbers were out of print. On a
second reading I found something to criticize
in the style, and perhaps the construction
laboured under some defects ; but they were
still absorbing. Who wrote them ? Somebody
connected with the pantomime stage, I suspect ;
and where can I get them ?

Which brings me back to Temple Grove and
to the recollection of the stories which certain
boys used to tell when we were out for walks
or marching round and round the playground at

extra drill. They went on for days, and were of thrilling interest. I can't recall a single episode, but I do know that some of the boys who were best at telling them were quite stupid in other ways, and I am sure that by the time they were sixteen they could no more have made up a romance than flown. Everybody must remember that he or some of his friends had this odd evanescent power at the age I speak of.

As at *Crichton House*, so at Temple Grove, the custom was that at some time on Sunday afternoon Mr. Edgar or another master read aloud to the junior boys assembled in the big schoolroom a work of an improving character. Certainly Adams's *Sacred Allegories* and probably Wilberforce's *Agathos and other Sunday Stories* were brought out on these occasions ; it was the most old-fashioned proceeding that prevailed at the school. The First Class had a superior entertainment, as was but right, for to them Waterfield himself read aloud, in the drawing-room. This we very much enjoyed ; to see Waterfield in a milder light, to feel that he unbent to some slight extent, was highly interesting. Besides, he was a very good reader. Stanley's *Lectures on the Jewish Church*, Farrar's *Life of Christ* (in which I remember his sharply criticising faults of taste) and the *Pilgrim's Progress* were the books I heard him read. Some of us who knew the text of the *Pilgrim* were agog to see whether in the episode of Doubting Castle he would give

us the author's words and say, " that lock went
damnable hard." When he came to the point,
he checked slightly, and said "desperate hard."

Waterfield was Olympian both in appearance
and manner, and could discharge his bolts
with stunning force and unexpectedness. One
instance came home to me most painfully ; it
needs a preliminary explanation of two technical
terms, which is tiresome, but I cannot omit it.
First, on rare and very much prized occasions
the " evening was given," that is, evening school
was remitted, and for that hour or more there
was pandemonium in the big schoolroom, or
out of doors. Secondly, the common form of
punishment was the " daily list " : this meant
writing every day a page of copybook to be signed
by the writing master, and also an hour's extra
drill of walking round and round the playground
in fours under the sergeant's eye. Very well ;
one day (Lord) Grey (of Fallodon) and I, as
first and second in the school, were persuaded by
our friends to go to Waterfield and ask for the
evening. Now we had both been reported to him
for talking in the bedroom the night before ; but
we didn't know it, or hadn't taken the matron's
threat seriously. And when, confronting Waterfield in his study, we said : " Please, Sir, may
we have the evening to-night ? " his eye flashed
(as nobody else's eye ever did) and he said : " No,
you mayn't have the evening, but I'll tell you
what you *may* do : you may both of you go on

the Double Daily List till further notice."
Blasted by the stroke, we retired to a diet of two
copies per diem and two hours' extra drill.

Arthur Benson has described the writing
master whom I have mentioned with relish and
also with accuracy, but I am tempted to add a
little detail.

Mr. Prior's (why not give him his true name ?)
terror of Waterfield and assumption of vast
importance when dealing with the small boys
made him a richly comic figure to us ; but I
imagine that in his own circle he himself was
something of a humorist. I can't account otherwise for his obvious delight in making up
incredible romances about himself, which he
retailed to us when we were out for school walks
of a winter afternoon. He would be in charge
of the quite small boys. Fixed in my mind is a
fragment of one of his sagas, told with great
solemnity, of adventures which befell him when
staying at the castle of his wealthy uncle in the
North of England. He was returning from a
long day's shooting over the wide estate, when in
a narrow lane he encountered, to his great
surprise, a large and formidable dragon. No
doubt the combat was described, but I only
retain the concluding phrase : " Providentially
I was enabled to slay the terrible creature." It
would not have been judicious to throw doubt
on any of these narratives, or, next time you
asked Mr. Prior to sign a copy for you, there was

a possibility that you might have it returned on your hands. So, at least, we said, but I hope we were unjust.

A word about games, as played at Temple Grove. They were compulsory, but nobody told us how to play them. The standard of football may be judged from the fact that for thirty years or so I imagined and always said we played the Association game there. I am now told by one who should know, that it was Rugby. As to cricket, I know that as Captain of the School I was also Captain of the Second Eleven ; but this circumstance is only eloquent to my contemporaries. I don't think there was a " cricket master."

Among minor pastimes, that of conquerors (conkers) was very prominent in the chestnut season. The seasoned chestnut, oiled with immense care and strung on a leather boot-lace might last over more than one autumn, and since he took to himself all the scores of the chestnuts which he killed, he might attain the rank of a " thousander." Once, when I was at the top of the School, I discovered a plot, hatched by three of the smallest boys in the conqueror season, that they would run away to the home of one of them where large horse-chestnuts grew, and collect chestnuts, for an orgy of unexampled richness. I am afraid I divulged it.

When I left Temple Grove for Eton it was with a very miscellaneous stock of general information and plenty of hobbies in the bookish line ; I collected martyrdoms of Saints—the more atrocious the better—and Biblical legends, and by gifts of friends and purchase had accumulated a number of odd classics, such as Aelian. A happy chance threw some second-hand book catalogues—of David Nutt and Elijah Johnson—in my way, and from them I learnt names of obscure authors, all of whom it was my ambition —for no definite reason—to read. At this time, in fact, all antique knowledge seemed immensely desirable ; and so did what I called Archaeology, which meant exploring every accessible church in the holidays and writing copious notes on everything I saw. It all sounds dreadfully priggish, and I have no doubt my Divinity papers at Temple Grove and my Sunday Questions at Eton were a sad blend of ignorance and blobs of misplaced erudition ; but to me it was all fresh and delightful. Nothing could be more inspiriting than to discover that St. Livinus had his tongue cut out and was beheaded, or that David's mother was called Nitzeneth.

III

AND now we approach Eton in earnest ; and the day in September of 1876 when my father and I entered the drawing-room of Mr. H. E. Luxmoore and I first saw my tutor. I am not going to panegyrize or even to describe ; my tutor would not like it ; and I am daily thankful that he is on the spot to let me know that he would not. All I will say is that that is one of the very few pivot days of my life.

The externals of the introduction to school life have been worn threadbare by writers ; even if they had not, I cannot recall the first days at all minutely. The young Colleger is admitted by the Provost on the first possible day, and not till then does he put on his gown ; and I think I do remember that little ceremony in the College Library. I ought to do so, for at that moment I effectively became a scholar of Eton and could begin to write my name as James, K.S.

What are the chief things that come back ? The taking possession of my stall in Chamber (a corner stall, it was, at the North-West), and of the many new objects now owned for the first time, an arm-chair, a burry, a bath, and what not—let alone an entirely new costume. My stall, I soon discovered, had this advantage over others, that it was next to the gaslight at the end of Chamber which was alight all night, and that I could sit on the top of my bed and read, long after other people were asleep. Here is an odd little phenomenon which I noticed at those hours. If one boy began talking in his sleep, the infection was sure to run all round Chamber. It had an uncanny effect ; one could never hear what they said, there was merely a curious oppressed babbling.

The first time of going into school is another memory that has not quite vanished, chiefly because of the anxiety attending it. We did not know very well where the schoolroom was, or whom we should find there. When discovered it proved to be a small building rather like a Dissenting Chapel, in Gasworks Lane (it no longer exists), and he who presided there was H. G. Wintle, the best of men, as we soon discovered. He was tall, sharp-nosed, rosy-faced, with spectacles and black whiskers ; we told each other he was like Verdant Green. I have often wondered what led him to ask us in our first set of Sunday Questions, " What is meant by ' Cadmi nigellae filiae ' ? " (*Ans.* The letters of the alphabet ; the quotation is from the poet Ausonius.)

Since I began upon this section, I have read again Mr. Eric Parker's *Eton in the Eighties*, and there I find the life of the young Colleger portrayed with such truthfulness and such charm that I feel it has been done, for my generation, once for all. Mr. Parker, it is true, did not come to Eton till 1883, and I left in '82 ; but the conditions he describes are those of my time, and I simply cannot set out to write the whole story over again. The framework of life changed hardly at all between my day and his, and I shall not spend any time on that. But the *personnel*, of course, varied very much, and, besides that, Eton allows the days to be spent in many ways according to the taste and fancy of the spender. *Personnel*, then, and pursuits may be allowed a space here.

The Sixth Form of my first years contained Harmer, Lowry, Burrows, H. C. Goodhart, Arthur Ryle, Tatham *ma*. In the upper parts of College were R. H. Macaulay, Spring Rice (Cecil), J. K. Stephen, Wilson, Wellesley, Inge, C. M. Smith, Benson, Tatham *mi*., the Macnaghtens, White Thomson (R. W.), Stanley Leathes. Every evening at the end of Prayers the list was called over. The last Election sat and saw all the great and good file out, and for many years the College list of one's first half remained printed on the brain. It is the rule that to Chamber in any year the sixteen boys who compose Sixth Form and Liberty appear to be of unapproachable greatness ; but on mature reflection I do think ours were an uncommon lot. So were their immediate forbears, of whom were

E.K.   c

Herbert Ryle, Welldon, A. H. Cooke, Reginald Smith.

Fagging. Old family friendship with the Ryles was responsible for Arthur Ryle's choice of me as his fag. I doubt if it spelt happiness (is not this the taking phrase ?) for him. Some time passed ere I learned for certain that water must be *actually boiling* before tea is made with it. But not more than once did I make his toast in the gas and scrape it ; for the fagmaster can at once ascertain if this has been done by holding the toast over the tablecloth and tapping it ; blacks which have been driven into it by the scraping fall out and betray you, and gas leaves a flavour. Ryle must soon have realized that it would not do to trust me with any cookery that demanded skill. So my responsibilities were confined to his tea and toast, calling him for early school, bath-filling and emptying, and miscellaneous errands. In all other ways I was the gainer, for he was very kind and patient, let me do my work in his room of an evening, and when I stayed out—poisoned—for some time in my first half, prescribed *Vanity Fair*, thereby doing me inestimable service.

He must himself have been away from Eton at another time, for I certainly fagged for Cecil Spring Rice for a season, and have kind memories of that also. It was particularly interesting, when one was at work in the rooms of the great, to hear their conversation. I remember absolutely nothing about it, but I know they never said anything they ought not in my hearing ; and they administered justice in Chamber and the lower part of College very carefully.

Pursuits and pastimes.   Parker, K.S., did all the normal things and several that were not.   He fished, birds'-nested, and bug-hunted, and describes the proceedings in terms that make the mouth water.   Nobody has a keener eye for the Eton landscape at all seasons of the year.   He is also the *vates sacer* of the Shooting Eight, and of the Beagles.   The Wall he celebrates nobly, and the Field ; the River too in certain aspects.   To Cricket and Fives his allegiance is sound, but they fill a smaller space in his pages.   From him, however, you may learn who were the heroes in the several fields—the princes of the provinces— in my time and his.   Such knowledge is too wonderful and excellent for me : I not only cannot, but never did, attain unto it.

The only game I ever really cared about, or was any use at, was the Wall : it gave me my one quasi-colour as Twelfth Man in 1882.   I shall always say when occasion offers that but for a bad knee and a crumpled ear—both accruing from friction against the Wall (I still have the ear)—I should have played for College that year.   Whether that is so probably no one now living can tell, but I *was* a respectable Wall, and I did understand and enjoy the game.   Nowadays, when custom calls me to walk up and down inside the ropes with the Head Master on St. Andrew's Day, I sigh to think how little I remember of the inwardness of the Rules : they cannot, indeed, be kept in the mind unless you are constantly playing or umpiring in the game.

There was a great deal to be done in the football half by the young Colleger. Two games had to be learnt—Field and Wall—from the start. In the Field game nobody told you what to do, but they were very free in telling you that what you did was wrong. At the Wall, systematic instruction was imparted. My recollection is that in the early years, what with Chamber Field and Wall, and Lower College ditto, if you fulfilled all your engagements, there were two games to be played on every week-day except Friday—eleven in all ; but that there were very few weeks in which pupil-room or something of the kind did not cut off one or two of these. I went through with it, *tant bien que mal*, and have been profoundly thankful ever since that I was made to do it, though I never cared for the Field game.

So much for the winter half. In the Easter half there was nothing to worry about out of doors : *I practically never played Fives !* It was a great business to get a court, and I had no reason to think I should make much of the game. Then the Summer, and Cricket. Perhaps, being large, I might have been made into a useful wetbob (I don't regret that I wasn't), but the charges of £2 10s. for a *chance* (any boat available) and £5 for a *lock-up* (a boat reserved for your use) were prohibitive. So Cricket, represented by Chamber Game, was the dish provided. This again was to my physical (and doubtless moral) advantage, for it kept me out of doors for, say, five evenings out of six in the week. But that it was an amusement I never discovered ; my innings was a form—a shortened form—of service that must be gone through ; fielding a salutary discipline, keeping intellectual pride in its due place. Bowling? Well, that formed no part of the picture. Thank Heaven, there were no nets to be practised at, at prescribed seasons. And yet I don't know that I ought to say that, for that penance would have been accompanied by instruction, as it is now, and I might possibly have learnt something about the defence of the wicket.

This sums up the orthodox pastimes of the year. Honestly I do not believe I cherished any ambitions about any one of them, unless it were the Wall. More confessions are to come. By the time I left I suppose I knew all the house colours and a good many of the wearers of them by sight, for I moved among them. But in the early days I was reduced to a great deal of subterfuge and hypocrisy, pretending to know by sight the Captain of the Boats, of the Eleven, and the Keepers of the Field, as all the rest of my Election did : *whereas in fact I did not know them*, nor, in any but the most obvious cases, the colours they wore.

All the same, though an " unrepentant Sap," I was by no means a recluse.   I believe I made the best of both worlds, and led a healthy life, and, when things were going smoothly in pupil-room and in school and in College, I know it was a very cheerful one.

The collection of books in Tea-room, called College Library, contained the whole works of Dickens, which were not on our shelves at home. Upon these I fastened like a leech, and mastered them all, with the exception of the *Child's History of England*, which volume nobody but a convinced anti-Dickensian, whom it could not further injure, should be allowed to open.   Not many whole months can I have passed since without having recourse to some part of those writings.   I put Charles Dickens in the fore-front of the accessions to my pleasure which Eton gave, for it was wholly new.

Proximus accessit Thackeray: a long interval, never since bridged over, parted him from George Eliot.   There is an index to taste !   When I add Handel to the list of those who dwelt, and dwell, in my inner shrine, the measure is almost filled. No up-to-date person can be sufficiently interested now to ask what I think of Tennyson.

IV

IT seems neatest to insert here something more of what I have to say about hobbies. When Middle Division was reached (they call it C now!), the School Library, then in Weston's Yard and accessible in a minute from New Buildings, became my prey, and I found there such things as Walter Map's *de Nugis Curialium* and other Camden Society books, and Morris's *Earthly Paradise*—not to mention Mrs. Jameson and D'Agincourt to tell me about mediaeval art : the *Glossary of Architecture* with its beautiful woodcuts, and J. L. Petit's *Architectural Studies in France*, full of masterly sketches reproduced by something called the anastatic process. A few more halves, and Henry Babington Smith and I succeeded in wheedling the keys of the Fellows' Library out of Vice-Provost Dupuis, and for the first time we were able to handle actual manuscripts. I forget whether it was as boy or as undergraduate that I unearthed from a dusty top shelf the huge Anthem Book of the early years of the sixteenth century, written for Eton Chapel, and containing the only copies of a number of works by English composers. Though it is very imperfect, it is of first-class interest, musically.

The Eton collection of manuscripts was the first
in which I was able to browse untrammelled. The
liberty granted to me I hope I did not abuse :
it was another of the great gifts of Eton.

What about Music ?   Even if you did not take
regular music lessons, there was a good deal that
you could assimilate.   Among many other debts
I owe to Mr. Broadbent, Master in College for
most of my time, is this, that he made us begin
to learn the reading of tenor and bass parts in
hymn tunes.   From that we went on to the Sunday
Evening Musical, where (Sir Joseph) Barnby
took a miscellaneous body of masters and boys—
plus some choristers to strengthen the trebles—
through such classics as *Messiah*, *Elijah*, *Saul*,
Jephthah, Spohr's *Calvary*, *Theodora*.   Masters,
e.g. Arthur James, Johnny Lock, Stuart Donaldson, would be turned on to sing solos : and not
infrequently would be stopped and requested to
begin again.   This of course was pleasant, and
it is certain that the whole performance was
profitable.   How could one not be the better for
making intimate acquaintance with the chain of
choruses in *Saul* that begins with " How excellent
Thy Name, O Lord," and contains " Along the
Monster Atheist strode " ?

The School Concerts in my day were in College
Hall.   One was marred by College clock thinking
fit to strike continuously for a quarter of an hour
soon after we had begun.   I *suppose* it was an
accident : yet the argument in favour of design

is not negligible.   As in most school concerts, the ballads of the day were too conspicuous a feature, but there was good stuff as well.   Do I stultify myself by mentioning Barnett's *Ancient Mariner* in the same breath with " good stuff " ? I have not heard it since 1879, perhaps, but I do believe it is full of sterling, if simple, melody : to us it was most attractive.   That and the lovely singing of G. J. Maquay in *Acis and Galatea* remain with me.   Also the first production of the *Carmen Etonense* (Ainger and Barnby), which was instantly recognised as a thoroughly satisfactory school song.   Also the début of the Brass Band of the E.C.R.V., which nearly blew the front rows out of their seats with a composition called " Roses Underneath the Snow."

These things belonged to the experience of everybody.   There was another department of music cultivated by some of us with a good deal of enthusiasm—and that was Church music.   We took a vivid interest in the chants, hymns, and anthems in Chapel.   Arthur Benson, Hugh Childers, and yet more William Boyle were considerable connoisseurs of the Anglican double chant, especially as written by the earlier and more florid masters.   I ferreted out of a rubbish heap in the Chapel vestry a copy of the quarto Marshall & Bennett collection of about 1830, and another older book of chants by Jones : I am afraid my borrowing of them must be classed as one of my few thefts.   I gave both to Boyle, in whose hands they at least served a useful purpose, for they contributed to the King's College Chant-book which he compiled a few years later. Marshall & Bennett is full of the chants—some absurd, but many beautiful—of Beckwith, Crotch, Heathcote, Cooke, Ebdon, a number of which we committed to memory, and, seated round the high table in Hall on a summer evening, would warble in parts. We were very contemptuous of the Cathedral Chant-book used in Chapel, and then a recent work, because it eschewed all floridity, and gave no particulars about the composers of chants, heading them with such bare names as " Trent " or " Pymar," " as if the man was a dog ! " said Boyle indignantly. *Ancient & Modern* again came in for some very sharp criticism. In it were, and are, such hideous melodies as " O happy band of pilgrims " and " Through the night of doubt and sorrow " : and when it got hold of a tune with any richness, it cut out all the quavers, and made *Mount Ephraim* into " For thy dear saint, O Lord." I can understand the reaction it represented when I look at such tunes as *New Sabbath*: but that we had some right on our side and were justified in preferring *Wareham* (No. 63 *A. & M.*) to " Thy way, not mine, O Lord " by Maria Tiddeman, I am well assured. To judge from the appendix of tunes attached to *The Nebuly Coat*, I believe Mr. Meade Falkener would support me. The *English Hymnal* has

done something appreciable in the way of rein-
stating the good florid tunes : let me recommend
to the notice of future compilers those known as
Woodham, Langshaw, and *Warrington.*

It was Eton Chapel which first introduced me
to anthems as a regular feature : I had never been
at a cathedral service before. I succumbed at
once. Boys are impatient now of long anthems,
and are allowed to sit during that part of the
service—in accordance with a custom that prevails
almost everywhere else. I don't remember that
we thought twice about the trouble of standing
up, and certainly we took an unfeigned interest
in the Sunday anthems : nay, more, there was
quite an appreciable set who would look into
Chapel on weekday afternoons to hear a favourite.
Boyce's " O where shall wisdom be found ? " was
perhaps my own standard of excellence : Gounod's
" Here by Babylon's wave " marked the nadir.
When the latter was substituted at short notice
for the former by Barnby, there were resentful
letters in the *Chronicle !*

Chapel services in the form in which we knew
them were quite a recent institution in 1876,
but none of us suspected that. It was only after
the Public Schools Commission that the short
daily musical service took shape. The procession
of Sixth Form was no older. As to the six lay
clerks and sixteen choristers, they had come back
to us after a gap of about a century, perhaps. A
protracted study of the College Accounts has

failed to show me at what date it was that we took
to using the St. George's men and boys on Saints'
days and Sunday afternoons, and ceased to
maintain a choir of our own. It was an indefensible shirking of our duties, which the Commission
and the zeal of Mr. Wilder (as much as any one)
corrected. To us it seemed probable that the
lay clerks had always been where we saw them :
Orlando Christian (Thunderguts), Mellor, and
Smith (known, from a fancied resemblance to
the Master in College, as the Chignell-man)
were on the *Decani* side : Webb, Ogilvy, and
Darby on the *Cantoris.* Darby the alto was
known to us as the Goatsucker, and was popularly
believed to confine himself to whistling his
part. He was seldom if ever entrusted with a
solo. Ogilvy, at the season of Epiphany, had
his day out with " There beneath the lowly
shed They found the Heavenly Infant laid."
It occurred (I can't keep back these pedantic
details) in the course of an anthem called " In
the days of Herod the king," attributed to
Handel. This seemed strange : research—I
know not how much later—showed that the
anthem was a *pasticcio* made, I think, by J.
Pratt, organist of King's College—and that the
air performed by Ogilvy is from *Alexander
Balus*, where Cleopatra sings " Here amid the
shady woods, Fragrant flowers and crystal floods,
Taste, my soul, this charming seat, Love and
Glory's calm retreat. Hence, vain doubt and

idle fear, Joy and only Joy is here." This (a very delightful song) is followed in the original by the stage-direction *Enter Ruffians*, and a dreadfully funny chorus of " Mistaken Queen, you must with us ! " interspersed with shrieks from Cleopatra of " Help, help, O Isis ! Alexander, help ! " We can understand that Mr. Pratt found this unsuitable to the atmosphere of his designed anthem. However, these matters are rather for the Handelian specialist.

Barnby's choice of Sunday anthems was good and illuminating and elevating, and I think he succeeded in many cases in making the anthem serve its best purpose as an element in worship. With that sincere tribute I turn from Eton Chapel to St. George's. Does it seem a horribly un-boylike thing that, particularly in the Easter half, some of us should have rushed up to St. George's on every available after-four and sat through the service ? Yes, and not only in afternoons, but on occasional mornings as well ? It seemed quite natural to us : we did it because we really liked it (and came down the Hundred Steps, taking them *four* at a time, which I now think no mean feat). Sir George Elvey has my humble and hearty thanks for the music he allowed me to hear. Stroud's " Hear my prayer," Boyce's " By the waters of Babylon," and above all Michael Wise's " The ways of Zion "—all, you perceive, Lenten anthems—heard on dark afternoons in February or March, entranced me

as I sat in the stalls. How many people know
" The ways of Zion " ? It is for the most part
a dialogue between a bass and a treble : the only
chorus is a short piece occurring twice over. The
entry of the treble, " Is it nothing to you, all ye
that pass by ? " seems to me astonishingly beautiful, and the recurring duet of " For these things
I weep " has a poignant appeal. Michael Wise
perished, much as Marlowe is said to have done,
in a brawl, in 1687. I am sure he was a great
man, and I wish someone would edit, in a form
appreciable by me, his setting of the Lament
of David over Jonathan. His other accessible
anthems, " Awake up, my glory," and " Prepare
ye the way," are excellent in their kind, especially
the latter. Indeed, I know nothing better for
Christmas Eve. Dr. Mann, in the King's
College Anthem-book, credits him with " The
Lord is my shepherd," which I have much
desired to see : but alas ! even Dr. Mann cannot
now tell me where it is preserved. The St. George's
manuscript collection of chants was also admirable.
I copied it all out (it took several mornings)
for the benefit of Arthur Benson. But besides
music the building had a great deal to offer me :
there was glass—a fine collection of saints in the
west window—and there were scores of legendary
scenes carved on the stalls, some of which defy
interpretation to this day: even Sir William
Hope has confessed his doubts about them. All
these were meat for my note-books.

Unauthorized, we climbed the roofs, having found a ladder convenient in the Cloister : for some little time a mop which we mounted on the battlements remained to mark that modest achievement—at least, so we said : probably it was found and removed the same day. Altogether, St. George's and its *personnel* became very familiar : Dean Wellesley, Canons Courtenay, Anson, Wriothesley Russell, Hugh Pearson, Minor Canons Tahourdin and Sheppard : I shall not easily forget the Dean reading from Corinthians in a rasping voice and with evident relish, " But if they have anything to ask their husbands, let 'em ask 'em at 'ome : for it is a Shame for Women to speak in the Church."

What indefensible loquacity is this ! If it has any ulterior motive—beyond the pleasure of recalling very happy days—that motive is the wish to show that Eton can cater for many sorts of boys, athletic and bookish, and that Etonians will not interfere with those who choose to walk in byways, so long as they are not asked to say that the eccentric is the only right-minded person, and that their own beaten tracks are all wrong : and so long as they are sure that singularity is not assumed in the hope of attracting attention.

V

LET me return to the trivial chronicle of my Eton life. It had its ups and downs. Within my first fortnight I earned — most justly — a Georgic from Mr. Rumsey for cribbing some of my (mathematical) *extra work* from a neighbour in Chamber. The offence was not repeated, but my distaste for Mathematics was not lessened. During part of my first half I was ill—as I have said—and therefore next half became detached from the rest of my Election and found myself up to (Sir) Walter Durnford (my successor in the Provostship of King's). There was something of a fearful joy about this, for Mr. Durnford was the possessor of an extensive and richly coloured vocabulary : and when he did not like a thing, the division were left in no doubt. He did not like my way of doing maps—and I doubt if anyone else ever did : but nobody made their feelings clearer to me than he. I can still hear him proclaiming, too, that James, K.S., must get his hair cut before five o'clock school. More placid were the halves I spent in the schoolrooms of Messrs. Cameron, John Cole, and Ainger. Cameron gave Exemptions, written on small bits of paper, for good performances, three of which got you off the next punishment you might incur for being late or any offence that was not serious. They were of great use to persons who disliked getting up for early school as much as I did. In Johnny Cole's division you might pursue what peaceful studies you liked, unquestioned, if in other respects you did what was required, and did not talk in school. From Ainger I must have learnt a great deal. With him there was dignity and quiet, and ripples of humour, and, generally speaking, an atmosphere which taught self-respect. Next in the upward progress came Edward Austen Leigh. Again I must refer to Arthur Benson's sketch of him in *Memories and Friends* for an appreciative treatment. Mr. Eric Parker has written well of him, too : but nobody has got quite the correct text of Austen Leigh's proclamation to the division at the beginning of the half. I offer mine with confidence : it was committed to memory on the spot and (so long as my voice retained the power of reaching the upper G) repeated at frequent intervals. It ran thus (the pace, mind, is very deliberate), " To-morrow morning, at Halfpast Seven o'clock, you will come to my Pupil-room, all of you. And you will bring with you a Piece of Broad-rewled paper—a Piece of Blotting-paper " (movement on the part of the division towards the door, arrested by an exceeding bitter cry). " Go to your places, all of you! Holdsworth, go to your place! Every boy go to his place ! Perfect silence ! Not a word, not a syllable ! . . . And a Pin ! You may go." We studied Austen Leigh's delightful pronunciation and intonation with great care : we loved to hear him speak of a queshtion, a pidgin, a lagune : but do not let it be imagined that his division was one in which any liberties could be taken.

All schoolmasters afford some degree of pleasure to observing boys, by their catchwords and the little tricks that anyone inevitably picks up who speaks to the same audience day in and day out for weeks together. Almost everyone then at Eton, of any consideration, had his catchword, and we wrote them down on the wall by the fireplace in Upper Tea-room. I suppose everyone has his at this present speaking, and I must have got mine too, only I can't think what it is, and no boy will tell me.

From the pupil-room of Austen Leigh, where he took his division, I passed to that of Warre, where he took his. A peculiarity of his system was that he prescribed the use of Army Class note-books (large quarto size with marbled cover) and the copious taking of notes, which were to be divided into four columns. What each column was to contain I do not now recall : let us say that, after the manner of the Schoolmen, the notes were to be respectively literal, allegorical, tropological, and anagogical. Anyhow, they were liable to be inspected at uncertain intervals, and mine did not give unmixed satisfaction. There has always been some curious twist in the minds of my teachers and examiners—nay, of so-called friends as well—which leads them to disparage my handwriting: and yet at this period I modelled it very carefully upon that of my tutor: and yet—again—I believe *he* never really accepted whole-heartedly the responsibility (some might say the privilege) which, as I was not slow to point out to him, was his. But mine, like Mr. Pecksniff's, is a forgiving nature.

During the halves I spent up to Warre, two subjects of study came before us which to him were perfect godsends. They were the Fifth Odyssey with the Raft of Odysseus, and the Fifth Aeneid with the *Ludus Trojanus*. Ancient ship-building and military evolutions! What models, what hektographed diagrams, what disquisitions upon trenails and dowels (ἁρμονίαι and γόμφοι — I write without book, but you see I have not forgotten) were showered upon us! If at times we murmured at the slowness of our progress (for a line or two of text might occupy several schools), I hope we appreciated, as I do now, the genuine enthusiasm of Warre ; and I am sure that the pains he spent gave us a new idea of the actuality of the classics, and a glimpse of high ideals of work. The greatness of Warre remained to be revealed to the generality of boys when he became Head Master. Had one been his pupil, or a prominent wetbob or volunteer, or a colleague on the staff, one might have realised it even at the time of which I write. But in due course it *was* revealed, and abides.

From Warre to E. D. Stone—in Division II, in the First Hundred. Here the area widened : extras came in. With Broadbent we learnt Plato, with Rawlins Plautus, with Stone Philology out of a horrid little book whose name I forget. Plato and Plautus were real eye-openers, especially the former : the exposition of the *Republic*, the *Phaedo* and the *Apology* I do not doubt made a real difference in the minds of Broadbent's class. Rawlins took us through half a dozen plays of Plautus, reading a racy version of his own, and instilling as he went the rudiments of Latin etymology in a way which seemed to me quite admirable. And Stone, delicate scholar and delightful poet, made the ordinary schools— if works of Necessity—works of Profit and some degree of Pleasure as well.

On the threshold of the Head Master's division I pause to survey the other departments of Life and Work. Mathematics. I suffered under Rumsey and Eliseo Smith, suffered under Daman, Lock, and Rouse, less acutely under Dalton, Carter, Philip Williams, and not at all under Mozley or Hale. Ordinarily a Science Master, Hale had, under some stress or other, been allotted a Mathematical division in my last year but one. Arthur Benson, Harry Cust, and perhaps Tatham, were members of it. It was understood that the selection of our work was to rest with

ourselves. " What are you going to do, Cust ? "
" I was thinking of doing a little Algebra this
afternoon, Sir." " Very well." There was no
crude demand for results, and a deep tranquillity
pervaded the schoolroom. About the middle of
the half, Hale suddenly said, " I shall ask the
Head Master if we mayn't do something sensible,
instead of these stupid Mathematics." But I
think we continued to be nominally a mathematical division.

A greater wealth of incident marked the schools
spent in Mozley's room. " Sir, who got the
Newcastle in your last year here, Sir ? " " Be
quiet, you silly boy." " No, Sir, but who did,
Sir ? " " Silly boy, I did, as it happens."
" Oh, *Sir*, did you really, Sir ? " Pause. " Sir,
who got the Tomline (Mathematical Prize) in
your last year, Sir ? " " Stupid boy, be quiet :
go on with your work." " No, Sir, but I want
to know, really, Sir." " Well, I did : now get
on with your work." " Oh, Sir, did you really ?
You must be awfully clever, mustn't you, Sir ? "

This was said to be common form among the
lower divisions. Higher in the school the procedure
was more dignified. Shortly after I left, Mozley's
senior division formed themselves into a Club
called the Mozleian, of which the first Rule was
to this effect : " The Club shall meet at 5.15 p.m.
on whole schooldays in Mr. Mozley's schoolroom."
The appointed hour for Mathematical schools
was, it must be remembered, 5 p.m. Mr.

Mozley himself repaired to his room at 5 and awaited with some impatience the gathering of his division. At 5.15 they duly came, and were met with bitter reproaches. " Devereux, what is the meaning of this ? A quarter of an hour late!" etc., etc. Devereux, surprised and injured: " But, Sir, the Club doesn't *meet* till a quarter past. Surely you wouldn't like us to break the very first rule in the book ! " I don't know how far it was found practicable to adhere to the Rules, but I have always heard that the last school of the half was spent in passing votes of thanks to Mr. Mozley for the very able way in which he had presided over the meetings of the Club during the past session.

Daman was characterized in my mind by a tireless persistency in what he (rightly, no doubt) considered well-doing. " Listen to this, Churchill: *a* equals 4 : *a* plus *b* equals 6. Therefore *b* equals 2. Do you understand that, Churchill ? " Churchill (F. E.): " No, Sir." " Very well, let us try again : *a* equals 4, *a* plus *b* equals 6 : therefore *b* equals 2. Do you understand that, Churchill ? " " No, Sir." " Very well. . . . . *da capo.*

The Revd. C. J. Eliseo Smith, an admirable pianist, has left little mark on my mind as a teacher, but is the hero of a story for which my tutor is my unimpeachable authority. It is the evening of the first day of the Winchester Match, which is being played at Eton. Stumps have been drawn, and Mr. Smith, bearded, spectacled, frock-coated, is making his way placidly homeward towards Slough. He is met by an enthusiastic Old Wykehamist, arriving late on the scene from Slough Station. Recognizing that Mr. Smith must be an Eton Master, the Wykehamist accosts him excitedly. " I beg your pardon, Sir, but could you tell me how the match is going ? " " The match ? Oh, it's over ! " " Over, on the first day ! Good gracious ! Do tell me who won ! " " I believe *neither* side succeeded in securing the requisite number of runs."

Through the entrancing realms of Science we were piloted by Hale, Drew, Madan, Carpenter. A demonstration of Hale's was orally preserved. It is difficult to see what truth it can have illustrated, but here it is. Hale had kept some animal organism in a bottle of liquid for a long time. Then he examined the vessel. The organism had entirely disappeared and the liquid, he was supposed to have said, " was as clear as crystal ; but by Jove, boys, it stunk like blazes." Drew, we understood, had occupied an important position as Resident in a Native State in India, where he had power of life and death. A very amiable man he was, and taught me some rudiments of Geology which have not wholly faded, but to describe him as having retained at Eton any powers that could be called disciplinary, let alone autocratic, would be unmeaning flattery.

Madan was conceived of as a man without human
passions. He would say in an even voice to the
laboratory assistant : " Marshall, you have a
baby." " Yes, Sir." " Bring it to me at ten
o'clock to-morrow morning : I require it for the
purposes of an experiment"; and Marshall
knew better than to disobey. From Carpenter I
derived knowledge about the steam-engine, about
Botany, and elementary Physics, and I am sure he
was a good and lucid teacher. But as a warning
to scientists I must record how a question of
mine, to which I really desired an answer, was
met by him. " Sir, what *is* the difference
between a frog and a toad ? " " Well, *that's*
perfectly simple : one's *Rana* and the other's
Bufo." I am convinced there must be a better
solution than that.

German was an Extra which I did with the aged
Griebel in his rooms up town. What I acquired
lay dormant until the necessity of using German
books at Cambridge revived it. Italian was also
an Extra : that I did with the yet more aged
Cavaliere Volpe, who used to come down from
town for the purpose, assume his cap and gown
at Williams's shop, and await me—his sole pupil—
in the Head Master's Chambers : Madame Volpe,
who always came with him to take care of him,
remaining meanwhile in the recesses of Williams's,
whither, as I remember, I used to conduct the
old gentleman at the end of the lesson. The
French, which my mother taught us at home

(she was born and brought up at Tours), was never a difficulty. I daresay it did not advance very much at Eton, but it did not recede.

My blessing upon the hobbies which in all these years took up bits of the half and holidays, and upon those who encouraged me in them! Sometimes I would birdsnest or bug-hunt, as assessor or accessory only to my friend and messmate H. Wood ; often attend on his organ practices in the music room in New Schools, for he was an accomplished musician ; often explore the country : Stoke Poges, the Beeches, Langley, where we thumbed the Kederminster Library attached to the church, and I copied out the catalogue of it. Once, with leave off an absence, we got as far as Shottesbrooke, the best Decorated church in Berks, which must be ten miles off.

Then there were the literary hobbies. And here must be set down correctly the history of the extinction of a promising Orientalist. Having bought of Elijah Johnson for seven or eight shillings a copy of Dillmann's *Chrestomathia Aethiopica* (or Ethiopic Reading Book), I proceeded to investigate the language. The first item in the volume was an apocryphal Book of Baruch, known to experts now as the *Rest of the Words of Baruch*, or the *Paraleipomena of Jeremiah*. Already anything like a fresh apocryphal book was meat and drink to me, and I succeeded in stimulating an interest in the mind of Ion

Thynne also, who was of my Election.   Together we made an English version of Baruch—a book full of incident, of which the gist may be read in my *Old Testament Legends* (Longmans—price I forget what), and, greatly elated by our performance, we agreed that it would be a worthy offering to Queen Victoria.   We therefore wrote a very polite letter to Her Majesty, beseeching her to accept the Dedication of our work ; and posted it on an early day in 1879.   Alas ! Sir Henry Ponsonby intercepted the letter, and sent it to Dr. Hornby, intimating, I believe, that we should be the better for some personal correction.   That suggestion, however, was not followed up.   Only verbally were our foolishness and impertinence pointed out to us.   The world of scholars had to wait for some ten years before Dr. Rendel Harris produced a readable edition of the *Rest of the Words of Baruch*.   There is the true version of an incident on which I have often been challenged. People have asked me, " Is it true that you translated a Coptic Gospel when you were at Eton ? " for there seems to be a widespread inability to distinguish between Coptic and Ethiopic, whereas the latter is a Semitic language, and the former—well, is not.

VI

BEHOLD my Election now, in September of
1880, taking our places in the Head Master's
division, in that august room at the north end
of Upper School, hung with casts of ancient
sculptures and antiquated prints of Rome and
plans of the classical theatre, and emblazoned with
names of Newcastle scholars and medallists.

In the midst is the octagonal table at which the
Head Master sits. The left side as you enter is
occupied with the two rows of seats and desks of
the Collegers, the Captain being in the front row
nearest the Head Master. On the right sit the
Oppidans in like order. The Block is behind the
Head Master on that side. There are sixteen
boys on each side. Ten Collegers and ten
Oppidans constitute Sixth Form. The next
six Collegers are known as Liberty, because they
have the power of fagging. We do not speak of
Oppidan Liberty, for that is unmeaning : every
Oppidan in Upper Division may fag.

We are a sedate body. Hornby has his regular
customs of calling upon us to construe. He begins
where he will, and that is the only uncertainty
that awaits us. We are sure that, once started,
the process will be continuous. The next boys

43

will be put on, as they sit: there will be no dodging about, and we can calculate with an approach to certainty whether he will get as far as us. He seldom puts on Collegers and Oppidans in the same school. So, on a hot summer afternoon, or a dark winter one, at five o'clock, some of the occupants of the back benches sink, it is to be feared, into unconsciousness. I recall one such winter day when Hornby was asking us successively if we meant to compete for the Prince Consort's Prize, and (General) Hugh Fitton (D.S.O.) was wrapped in slumber, in the darkest corner, and neighbours either could not or would not disturb him. "Fitton," said the gentle, melodious voice : and again "Fitton" : and a third time "Fitton!" Fitton sprang to his feet—he was of enormous height—and began reading out with every appearance of interest that portion of Horace, we will say, which he supposed we might have reached. "No!" said the voice, "I was askin' whether you were goin' in for the Prince Consort's Prize. I'm afraid you weren't attendin', Fitton. Si' down."

I said we were a sedate body, and that is in the main true : but I must confess there were days every now and then when Another occupied Hornby's chair—one under whom we felt that some deviation from routine was permissible. One game, restricted to these occasions, was to construct a triumphal arch of quill pens, one stuck into another, over the entrance door.

The two ends were begun simultaneously on the Colleger and Oppidan seats nearest the door and finally joined up at the apex of the arch. Then it would fall over and on to the table, and perhaps attract the teacher's attention for the first time, and evoke protests. It was desirable, of course, to get it finished quietly : it didn't much matter what happened after that. Hugessen, at one of these schools, drew a very telling portrait of the presiding master on a piece of broad-rule and inserted it in one of the picture frames near his seat. When it was seen, there was an angry cry, directed at the boy just beneath. " Williams ! What do you mean by this ! I shall write a letter to your tutor, couched in very strong terms. Is it worthy ? " The accused was, to be sure, very much shocked by the baseless charge. One is glad to think that Hugessen did not suffer him to remain under it long. Rising in his place, he said : " Sir, I cannot tell a lie. I did it, with my little hatchet." The confession was so flabbergasting that the incident closed. I have other visions of a school being taken under like conditions in the Head Master's Chambers— a saying lesson,—and of H. B. Smith wandering about, opening a desk and finding a number of confiscated pistol cartridges, which he dropped by relays into the fire just behind the magisterial chair, with results very discomposing to us all, but most to the occupant. We were asked again, " Is it worthy ? " and I am bound to say that on a long view it was not. But the view of the moment was that these were good diversions, and that anyhow it was " up to " the man in charge to stop them.

We were very happy up to Hornby, and loved him dearly. Though he appeared to be passionless, he interested us in our work. It seemed to gain in dignity from the way in which it was treated. Those were happy weeks in which one was Sixth Form Praepostor. One Colleger and one Oppidan officiated at a time. The Captains, and perhaps the two next, if they were lucky, got two Praepostorships in the half. During that week you went into early school on Monday and to Chapel every day, and, I think, to Extras and Mathematics, but not into other schools. Your chief business was to go round the Divisions, open the door and say "Is Blank in this Division ?" The Master answers " Yes " : you reply " He's to stay," and depart. Blank does not literally stay. But why dwell upon his actual fate ? It is known to Etonians, and would only pain and terrify the humanitarian.

In the Winter and Easter halves, there were and are six sets of Speeches in Upper School, on three Saturday mornings in each half : in Summer there were only the Fourth of June Speeches, for those at Election had died out ere my time. These ordinary Speeches were attended by the Provost, Vice-Provost, any Fellows who were available, Head Master, Lower Master, and First Hundred.

Those members of Sixth Form who were to take part in any week were excused verses, and were said to skip. So were the Praepostors.

" I haven't had your verses, have I ? " says Hornby. " No, Sir, I'm skipping this week." " Skippin' ? Didn't you skip last week ? " " Did I, Sir ? " " Yes : I think there's been too much skippin' lately : I can't have boys skippin' week after week in this way."

About Speeches themselves I do not remember very much : the *Chronicle* tells what they were. I recollect speaking *Ibam forte via sacra* and *Rejected Addresses* (the Crabbe parody), and also acting as prompter to E. M. Wood, who had but imperfectly mastered the Agincourt speech of Henry V. When we got to " Harry the King, Bedford," there was a pause. *Prompter* : " and Exeter." *Speaker* : " and Exeter." *Pause. Prompter* : " Warwick and Talbot." *Speaker* : " Warwick and—— " *Prompter* : " Talbot." *Speaker* : " and Talbot." *Pause. Prompter* : " Salisbury." *Speaker* : " Salisbury." *Prompter* : " and Gloucester." *Speaker* : " and Gloucester."

Prompter might have continued *ad libitum* with Worcester, Hereford, Oxford, Cambridge, Manchester, Liverpool, etc., etc. But the situation was already too embarrassing for all parties.

Life in Division I was, you will have gathered, placid, but a jolt occured every now and then. A vignette of the same E. M. Wood comes back to me. A winter morning after early school : a room in Sixth Form Passage. The rest of the mess are at breakfast : E. M. Wood, in a great-coat and gown (he was a chilly subject), hurries in rather late, looking like nothing but a borogove. The end of his nose is red and has the singular property of moving or seeming to move apart from the rest. Without a word he seizes the brown teapot from the table and draws an arm-chair to the fire, over which he crouches (like Mrs. Fibbitson, *vide David Copperfield*,) hugging the teapot to his bosom, a prey to the deepest gloom. Somebody at the table wants it and wrests it from him : he utters an inarticulate cry of intense agony and repossesses himself of the teapot. " What's the matter ? " someone says at last ; the dreary answer comes back, " Nailed cribbing Sunday Q's."

I don't know what penalty this crime would entail, for I never practised it. Shirking early school, however, had its regular tariff, which memory puts at two hundred lines. Whether two hundred or four hundred or a Georgic, it was a small price to pay for the pleasure of saying to oneself on a particularly dark cold morning : " Well, I'm blowed if I'll go into school," and turning over in bed. But that liberty could not be taken more than twice, I should say, in one half.

The delights of life in College increased rapidly as one rose in the school and began to

take part in running the show. Hitherto you
had known the adjacent Elections to your own,
above and below, pretty well ; now your acquaintance extended as far upward as you chose. It
was in those years that I became really familiar
with Arthur Benson, Remington White-Thomson,
Tatham, Boyle, E. M. Wood, in the upper
regions. Fitton, Bartlett, L. J. White-Thomson
(Bishop of Ely), Hugessen (Lord Brabourne),
Frank Marchant, were prominent figures just
below, with Childers, R. S. de Havilland, H. B.
Smith, just above, who almost counted in our
Election. Outside College, too, one's circle was
increasing. In your early years at Eton, whether
you are Colleger or Oppidan, there is not much
communication between house and house. Neighbourhood in school and in games does something :
I generally found several Oppidans in my division
whom I liked, but I shouldn't have thought of
going out for a walk with them on Sunday.
But when you reach First Hundred and begin to
be elected to School Societies you may make
friends anywhere, for you meet boys on fresh and
different terms. Still, on a Colleger, College, so
much larger than any house, has the first call.
And besides, when can you see anything of your
Oppidan friends in winter, when lock-up is at
five ? I always say that the quintessence of
indoor Eton life was best tasted on a Saturday
evening in the Winter half. Suppose lock-up,
as I said, at five : tea over : no private business to

take you out to your tutor's : no meeting of a
Society, nor lecture : a long lie in prospect. You
put on a blazer or a change coat and repair to some
familiar room in Sixth Form Passage or the Tower,
and there you sit by the fire with three or four
people whom you really like, and till nine o'clock
prayers you talk. Very probably your talk is
largely gossip ; you con over, lovingly or otherwise, the little ways of your masters and your
contemporaries ; but if you are bookish, and in
the mood, there is no prejudice against your
discussing books. Certainly, nobody expects you
to spend the whole time in speculation as to who
will get what colours and whether he ought to ;
nor are you bound to that high plane on which the
heroes of Farrar's *Julian Home* seem to have
moved. After all, what mattered more than the
words said was the sense of *bien-être* and comfortable affection which pervaded the room. It was
of course in such coteries that the jokes of the
community were hatched, and the mythology
with which the authorities were always decorated
was formed. Benson had clearly seen that
Hornby at early school had nothing on under his
cassock and preacher's gown but a night-gown :
that in Chapel Miss Blank was in the habit of
suspending herself by her nose from the book-
ledge when other people were kneeling. Or we
recalled how on a summer's day when Dalton's
schoolroom door stood open, those sitting near it
perceived a drunken man lurching uncertainly

about outside, and silently beckoned him in. The stranger entered quietly enough, and something in the atmosphere suggested to him that he was in a place of worship and that some religious ceremony was being performed ; and very decorously he knelt down and held his hat before his face for some moments. Then it was that Dalton perceived him and with a hoarse cry of " Who's that ? Is he drunk ? Let me get at him," made an ugly rush, and the poor man fled.

(Here it would be possible, if I could think of them, to insert a number of stray fragments of myth, but nothing suitable comes to hand. Perhaps I ought to direct the printers to leave a blank page for MS insertions by readers. On the whole, I think this Tristram-Shandy-like trick will be better avoided.)

At 8.30 (or 8.45, was it ?) the Praepostor would gravitate towards Hall to keep order at supper : and would mull a glass of beer by the simple process of putting a hot poker into it. It would then be offered to old Holderness, the College butler, with the words " Not the first glass of beer you've drunk in College Hall, Mr. Holderness," to which the response (invariable as in a Liturgy) was, " And I hope it won't be the last, Sir." Holderness ought to have been a mine of tradition, but we never really probed him ; we always played for his description of Dr. Balston, " ripe scholar—stiff as a poker— very good man, though." This was one of the things, not funny in themselves, which become exquisitely amusing by force of mere repetition. From Hall to Prayers, from Prayers to Sixth Form supper (on Saturday evenings, to be sure, there was a debate in College Pop, but I cannot delay upon that), which took place in Tea-room. There awaited us the cold joint, the tart, the Stilton and the beer. The tart—apple-pie really, as a rule— and the Stilton had to be brought across from Hall by the fag whose business it was that week. The Stilton was contributed in turn by each member of Sixth Form, which meant a tax of a pound at some time in your career. On rare occasions before supper there was an arraignment of small boys—or maybe large ones—who had been behaving ill : and there might be a " working off," that is, a caning : the term, peculiar to College, I doubt not comes from *Barnaby Rudge*, where Dennis the hangman always uses it to mean an execution. After supper we would indulge in song, sometimes : sometimes in parlour gymnastics : *e.g.*, place the forehead upon the ball of the poker held vertically on a fixed point in the floor and move round it six or more times ; then level the poker and charge at some object at the end of the room and see how near you can get to it.

The services of the praepostor were again required shortly before ten, to keep Chamber and see that the Captain thereof called out " Five minutes to " as a signal for silence, intended to make it easy for boys to say their prayers. Then, the praepostor and friends would keep the passages, Upper and Lower. Then bed. My room was in my last year the top Tower room, which has a staircase to itself. Of a summer night, when College is asleep, and there is but little traffic in the streets, you hear the rushing of Romney Weir, and, at midnight, the three great clocks : our own, in Lupton's Tower, strikes the quarters and the hour : the big one in the Castle quadrangle has a deep bell for the hour only : the Curfew Tower, where the bells of St. George's are, has more to say. When it has done the hour it sets off upon a psalm tune—that known as St. David's, " How blest the man who ne'er consents By ill advice to walk, Nor stands in sinners' ways nor sits Where men profanely talk." That is followed by a tinkling chime, which is the prettiest part, and thrice is the song repeated. It goes on at three, six and nine o'clock as well as twelve ; but unless you are in Windsor street just beneath it, you can never hear it but at midnight.

I don't know what I thought about when I listened to the Weir and the clocks and the chimes, and smelt the perfume of the lime-blossom in the Long Walk, but if I had been capable of writing poetry, I daresay I should have written it then. A still summer night in one's last half at Eton ! I ought to have been filled with great projects for the public good, and wonderings as to what I was going to be and do. But I am sure there was none of that, only a sense of how kind a mother Eton was, and how many people that I was fond of were about me.

VII

I CASUALLY mentioned School Societies just now : they deserve a page or two. There were the Literary, the Scientific, the Shakespeare, and Pop : in College, College Pop and College Reading Society. But Mr. Parker is the *locus classicus* for College Pop, and of the others few need detain me.

The Literary Society, in which I succeeded Arthur Benson as President, read papers and organized lectures. Twice I heard Ruskin, and twice Mr. Gladstone : Ruskin first on the English Lakes (at least that name occurred in the title), when he took occasion to deliver a tremendous denunciation of Gustave Doré : again, later, on the Bible of Amiens (the text of which will be found in *Our Fathers have told us*). This was illuminating. For the first time I learnt what might be read, and in what spirit, in the imagery of a great church : and what the thirteenth century had to say to the nineteenth. I say I then learnt it first : yet I doubt if in so saying I do justice to my tutor, who, a faithful disciple of Ruskin (and long Master of his Guild), had at the very least prepared my mind to absorb that lesson. During that lecture College clock struck nine, and Ruskin raised his hand to command silence, and listened, rapt, to the sound. No one felt it to be in any way absurd : some had a new value for College clock after they had seen a great man so moved by it.

Mr. Gladstone's lectures were both upon the subject of Homer (we said he pronounced it " Oomy "), and he ended the second of them with a glowing panegyric of Eton—" the queen of all the schools of all the world." I am sure this represented his true feelings. We were the more annoyed when within a few days he paid a visit to Wellington or Marlborough and contrasted their virtues with ours, to our disadvantage. But the most eloquent, the most ornate, that ever we listened to was that of F. W. H. Myers on Nelson. It is no use to forbid me to be fascinated by Myers's *St. Paul :* I have never found the spirit of an afternoon in Switzerland better caught than in some verses of his called *Simmenthal,* which begin :

> " Far off the old snows ever new
> With silver edges cleft the blue,
> Aloft, alone, divine."

And I am unimpressed if you tell me that his oration on Nelson was full of purple patches and cheap rhetoric. It was a stirring thing to hear.

The Literary Society was not of very old foundation. Mr. Curzon (Lord Curzon of Kedleston), when Captain of the Oppidans, was one of the early Presidents. Certainly he was the first who took his duties seriously. He procured a President's Book stamped with the Eton arms, in which successive officers were to write hints for those who came after : and he himself inaugurated it with a discourse of thirty or forty pages, chiefly dealing with the best method of hiring chairs for lectures. It is characterized by that wonderful attention to small detail and that unsparing industry which were conspicuous in his life's work. The Book, owing to the indolence of successors, did not fulfil its design. Arthur Benson, when he left Eton, took it to King's, intending to write something in it, and send it back. The something was eventually written—not much of it—and the Book was handed on to me, who had by that time come up to King's. With me (I apologize to everyone concerned) it remained until long after the Society had ceased to exist. I then returned it, and it was laid up in School Library. Curzon initiated a similar Book for Pop, and wrote a good deal in that, too : but it was not continued. A third, to which his contribution was perhaps the most voluminous of all, was concerned with the privileges and duties of the Captain of the Oppidans. This, I understand, was started before his time, and is still in use.

To Pop I was elected as President of the Literary Society, not on the score of athletic eminence. Pop was a delightful refuge ; it was a distinct pleasure too to be able to conduct one's correspondence on paper headed with " Eton Society " or POP in a monogram. Amusing also to read the old debate-books, with pages of Mr. Gladstone's writing. Speakers then, and in my time also, were supposed to write a *précis* of what they had said. These records dwindled in length as the debates came to form a less and less important part of the Society's life ; but at first they, and the wrangles that took place over Private Business, were made to fill scores of pages. " Good God, Sir," cried Mr. Holland, " what insanity is this ! " was the kind of outburst you met with now and again. The debates in my time were still weekly, taking place, I think, on Monday after four. The only one I have any recollection of was that in which I persuaded Hugessen to propose " That the promulgation of the Bulls *Execrabilis* and *Regnans in caelis* was an indefensible step on the part of the Pope." (I had been reading Robertson's *History of the Christian Church*—the volume in which the suppression of the Order of the Templars was narrated.) I supplied the proposer with some facts, and I myself may have been seconder (which in our parlance stood for opposer—a delightful idiom). Hargreaves, I remember, was reduced to saying that the Bulls seemed to have done a lot of damage, and it was very imprudent of the Pope to have let them out.

The Shakespeare Society was started in 1880-1 by the Cornishes and Frank Tarver. It met on Monday evenings at the Cornishes'. And still it flourishes under the presidency of my tutor : and still on Tuesday evenings, whenever I am able, I am thankful to be allowed, as an original member, to occupy a seat there and follow the text in the same dilapidated Globe Shakespeare which I used in 1880, when it yet possessed a cover, and the leaves at the beginning and end did not flake off one by one and have to be put into the middle of the volume for preservation. I ought to be able to remember the admirable reading of Frank Tarver and Mr. and Mrs. Cornish : but I confess I do not. In those days, the admixture of seniors and of ladies was larger than now, when, very rightly, active participation is confined (except when someone is unexpectedly absent) to the six Collegers and six Oppidans who are full members. Mrs. Tovey I do recollect, and her solemn emendations of passages which seemed to her a little too Elizabethan. As when she gave the following text of two well-known lines in *Macbeth* :

"I'd snatch the Bottle from its boneless gums
And dash it into fragments."

I credit her now with being conscious of the humour of it, but we did not at the time.

Once in June, when the Society broke up, Arthur Benson, Harry Cust, and I found it far too lovely a night for going straight home, and, with a breach of the trust reposed in us which I cannot defend, wandered up the Slough road, got over the Wall and roamed as far as Sixth Form Bench, where we sat and looked at the River and listened to the Guards' Band at the Castle playing the *Lost Chord* to Queen Victoria as she sat at her dinner. The *Lost Chord* may be a very meretricious piece of music, but the close of it, heard under those conditions, was extraordinarily appealing. It must have been, for me to recall it as I do in 1925. We went unpunished, but not undetected. As we turned homeward from Sheeps' Bridge, we were met by Rouse, smoking a nocturnal cigar, and he—who by accident or design played fast and loose with his h's—said to us, " Har the great gates not shut ? " We didn't know. " Then 'ow in the world did you come 'ere ? " We explained as well as we could and were sent home : but I have never forgotten the atmosphere of that June night.

Among scholastic pursuits the Newcastle took the foremost place. It filled up the chinks in the Easter half very completely. You read by yourself all the classics you could, and worked up one of the Gospels, the Acts, and General Divinity. When the day came, you repaired to School Library and did three papers a day. As a compensation you were allowed to be out for an hour after lock-up. On the third evening the list of the Select was published. Next

morning that body went again to School Library
at nine o'clock and found a copious breakfast
awaiting them. (The breakfast disappeared with
the Library : nobody could possibly breakfast
in New Schools.) There they sat, and one by
one were summoned upstairs to undergo a
short *viva voce* from the Examiners, who sat in a
small room with stuffed birds in it at the end of
the gallery. Later in that same morning the
result was given out.

Besides other advantages, the Newcastle
brought me one in particular. The first year
I was in[1] the Select my tutor took me and
another, J. A. Pixley, to France for a fortnight
in the summer holidays, and showed us Paris,
Bourges, Auxerre, and Nevers. That was a
boon not to be measured ; it was my introduction
to mediaeval glass and sculpture, but above all
to the sacred soil of France. Again in the Easter
holidays after I had become Newcastle Scholar,
he took me to Italy. Stuart Donaldson accompanied us. The two great features that time
were Florence and the Lakes. Pure enjoyment,
diversified by a crossing of the Simplon on the
return journey, when the diligence was held up
by a snowfall and we had to cross the top of
the pass in sledges. We were rather nearly
wiped out by an avalanche which came down
right over us. Hastily extricating ourselves,
we ran for the nearest shelter, which was luckily

---

[1] They say *on* the Select now : we didn't,

only a few hundred yards off, and waited there for a considerable time while more avalanches thundered over us. I have a vivid memory of getting up from under the first one, that knocked us over, and finding that my hand was planted on the very red and peeling face of a fat Frenchman who occupied a seat in our sledge. Vivid also is the image of that afternoon, when, having safely reached Brieg, we went and lay in a sunny meadow which was perfectly full of mole-crickets, and I was led to think how dreadful a place the world would be if mole-crickets were six times as large as they are.

But what is comparable, after all, to the very first day in France? We had done the really luxurious thing, sleeping at the Lord Warden at Dover before crossing; the Channel was a mill-pond : our ship was that odd double-bodied steamer associated with the name (I think) of Captain Bessemer. Then Calais towers and lighthouse : then the bestowing ourselves in the train, and the joy of reading from the window the mysterious inscriptions Lens-Somain, Frein à Vide, Amer Picon, and the rest. The passing of Abbeville and sighting the towers of St. Wulfram—the church of Longpont on the other side of the Somme valley—the great mass of Amiens—the thousand and one things that still make the train journey from Calais to Paris a delight to me. Does anybody, I wonder, share with me the thrill of pleasure with which on a bright August day I greet certain obscure stations between Calais and Boulogne : notably Rang-du-Fliers-Verton and Marquise-Rinxent ? But I fear there must be more anon of France : the present point is that I owe all the immense stock of pleasure and knowledge I have drawn from it to my tutor.

VIII

IT is a necessity laid upon nearly all writers of such recollections as mine that they should encumber their pages with long lists of names known or unknown to fame, and should write of poor So-and-so, who was killed in a motor accident, and dear old someone else, that " prince of good fellows " (a peculiarly odious phrase to me) who won the Pewter Cup at Windsor Races in 1867 with *Dilettante*, and never recovered from the consequent excitement. These chronicles do not make very good reading: the writers seem as little able as Shallow, J.P., to get away from the fact that a great many of their old acquaintance are dead, and that some of them came to sad ends: which, after all, has not much bearing on life at school.

Now I have reached the point at which it seems necessary to say something more of my contemporaries, and how am I going to avoid this Slough of Despond ? Only, I think, by restricting myself to the boy's point of view, who does not greatly trouble himself with speculations as to the destiny of those about him. When I ran errands for Harmer and Burrows, I did not say to myself, " These men will be Bishops.

I will therefore take pains to buy them the *best* buns I can find." Nor, later on, when I was on intimate terms with Arthur Benson, did I conceive of him as the future author of a whole shelf-ful of volumes. It may even have seemed likely that H. F. W. Tatham would be the more prominent. But Tatham was incurably unambitious. I do not think he even competed for a Trinity Fellowship. A man of impassive countenance and acute sense of humour, he was a dreadful neighbour when anything mirth-provoking happened in school or church or any other assembly where gravity had to be preserved. There would be a sharp nudge from his elbow in your ribs, and the bench would tremble under his massive form : but while you sighed and sobbed with the agony of suppressed laughter, he would only glance at you with pained surprise. Rather brutal I thought him when I first came across him, but he developed into the champion of all suffering things. " I like toads," he said, " they're dry and weak." He was very sympathetic, too, with cats. He told me how in the drawing-room of his home in London he picked up the family cat and carried her to the window and made her look out into the street. After contemplating the busy scene for a few seconds, she looked up at him and gave a heavy sigh. He put her back on the sofa. Either just before or just after he left Eton he got into the courts (in the holidays) for taking it out of someone who was ill-treating a dog—as the Vice-Provost has related. To him came the reward—which must be a very rare one—of finding a dead parrot in a lane somewhere near Eton Wick : known thereafter as Parrot Lane to his friends.

For Harry Cust I think we did prophesy a brilliant future. Nobody came nearer to the conception of the Admirable Crichton. An excellent Captain of the Oppidans, and of his House, a worker, the most shining of social successes, competent at games (what colours he had I don't remember), good-looking, a most facile speaker, a delightful actor : his *Puff* in the *Critic* on his last Fourth of June was a first-rate performance. He really was the expectancy and rose of the fair state. Any degree of intimacy with him at Eton was an honour and a delight.

Hugh Fitton, remembered by the generality as a great soldier, is thought of by me as an inexhaustibly humorous figure. He cultivated an elaborately courteous address : it may be exemplified in a scene with his tutor, Mr. Thackeray. The first set of Thackeray's pupils, including some of the best scholars—Macnaghten, Tatham, the White-Thomsons—are in pupil-room, engaged on Private Business, let us say Thucydides. Thackeray tells Fitton to go on translating.

Fitton (most politely) : " No, Mr. Thackeray, I must ask you to excuse me. This passage is one for which I have a special admiration, and I should be very sorry to give an inadequate rendering of it. Might I suggest that you should ask Macnaghten or Tatham to translate it ? I am sure the result would be far more satisfactory to all parties."

Thackeray: " No, no, Fitton, I can't have this absurd modesty. You must translate the passage."

Fitton : " No, indeed, Mr. Thackeray ; I must positively decline. In addition to other considerations, I am not very well just now, and my doctor tells me that any over-exertion of the brain would be highly prejudicial to me at this time."

I don't know how long the contest would continue : but I am informed that Fitton usually got his way ; and the Vice-Provost tells me that he and Tatham were not at all gratified by Fitton's high estimate of their attainments as expressed on these occasions.

There are two theatres of activity—out-of-door activity—which I have postponed: the River and the Corps. They did not, in fact, play much part in life at first. True, I did pass, in my first summer half, at Athens, but it was not often that one had a free afternoon to spend on the river. Bathing, however, was always a joy. Some people would go as far as to sacrifice the long lie on Sunday and go out to Athens : I can't say I ever did that ; bed was too precious.

But in a really hot season, after twelve, after four, *and* after six were not too much time to devote to the water. No hunger approached that which a good long bathe excited: an old man in a top hat and a white smock, who haunted about Athens, stanched it with a peculiar kind of cheese—as well as buns, the newer the better. Clad in a simple towel, one basked on the Acropolis and looked at the Castle shimmering in the heat, and, with the smell of the river in one's nose, was conscious of complete physical happiness. Of Boveney it is useless to attempt the praises after Mr. Parker. I have my regrets that it is no longer a School bathing place, but I recognize that it does take a long time for the poor boys to get there; also that the new iron contraption about the weir makes it less interesting than it was; lastly, that they have almost—perhaps quite—as good a substitute at Romney.

I fear most of my wet-bobbing was done with a view to a bathe. One did occasionally get to Surly Hall, but oftener only to Athens. I have manned—helped to man—a dry-bob eight, no doubt, when in Sixth Form: I have regularly done what had to be done in College sweepstakes. At water parties—the noble entertainments which Austen Leigh or Ainger would organize after Lord's—mine was not the weakest arm of those that urged the shallop down from Hedsor, or up from the Bells of Ouseley. Mem-

bers of the Eight have as good as said so. But
I must confess that it was pleasure and not glory
that I asked the River to give me, and he certainly
gave it.

It was in 1879, under the instigation and at the
expense of my eldest brother, who then came to
Eton as a Master, that—simultaneously with
him and the late J. D. Bourchier—I joined the
Corps—the E.C.R.V., now E.C.O.T.C. There
was an unsuspected Providence in this. You do
not need to be told what real greatness in the
political world Bourchier afterwards attained :
the only Eton Master who ever has had, or
one supposes ever will have, the postage stamps
of a nation emblazoned with his portrait. But
even I, who was an eye-witness, despair of being
able to tell you how little his talent for diplomacy
enabled him to cope with the manual exercise,
or to execute the simplest of military manœuvres.
Never did he fail to " charge swords as a rear-
rank man": always, when the word "Form fours
right " was given, he interpreted it as " Form
fours left." I call it a Providence which ordained
that he and I should join on the same day, for
it is certain that he diverted many a bolt which
must, but for his presence, have fallen on me.
Even as it was, Captain or Major Walter Durnford felt himself justified in saying (on parade)
at a later date, " If you wish to see a Monument
of Inefficiency, look at Lance-Corporal M. R.
James." I think I have mentioned before that

mine is a forgiving nature : but I could have reminded him that one is never at one's best on Monday mornings, and these directions to take ground on the right and what not are very irritating and confusing when one chances to be thinking of something else. With all drawbacks, the Corps contributed to my well-being and amusement. Field days were not felt to be oppressive. Camp was not a Work of Necessity : I only attended it once, at the end of my last half, when it softened the pangs of leaving. It was in Ashridge Park, in perfect weather : H. B. Smith and I had a tent to ourselves. We had a service on the Sunday in the Chapel of Ashridge House, and John Baring played the organ.

But on one occasion I behaved very ill in relation to the Corps. Hugessen, whose dislikes were no subject of concealment with him, disliked the Corps. He had a room off Upper Passage which commanded College Field. And it was his deplorable custom on Monday mornings in the summer, when the Corps paraded there, to summon his friends and emulate and indeed overpower the Band by beating baths with india-rubber siphons. Why I was not always on parade on these occasions I cannot tell; it is certain that I was wielding a siphon on one day when Quarter-Master Hale was suddenly detached to form a reconnoitring party and ascertain whence the vulgar sounds proceeded : for Dr. Warre, then in command, was justifiably enraged.

The net result was that Macnaghten, as Captain of the School, had to convey apologies to Warre, and that Hugessen remained wholly impenitent. The rest of us, I think, not.

Two other occasional forms of recreation, respectively legitimate and illicit, will be the last I inflict on you. The latter was roof-climbing, which has a strange fascination for the young. It included Chapel (when work was going on there and we had found where the key of the turret staircase was kept). That was in the day-time. Also Chamber roof. The chimneys of the rooms in Sixth Form Passage were then low, and it was possible to drop a brick into one and then come down and enter the room as casual visitors, and, like Mr. Pickwick, " gaze without a sigh upon the ruin we had made." Another phrase of Serjeant Buzfuz is almost equally applicable ; we might fairly be said to have " choked up the well and thrown ashes on the sward."

Cloister roofs were customarily visited on the night when the Newcastle Select came out : the expedition served to distract our minds. We got very dirty and caught bats. At one place at the N.E. corner of Schoolyard there is a piece of battlemented wall with nothing behind it : H. B. Smith was the only one of us who would cross this.

The legitimate occasional sport was skating. We had several hard winters, coupled with floods.

South Meadow was flooded and frozen in more than one January. There was room there for most of the School to play hockey. Ditton Park has a moat on which the Duke of Buccleuch kindly allowed the boys to skate: you could easily get there and back between absences. But the best was Virginia Water. Several times my tutor drove parties of us over. It was too big to be crowded, and you could either wander over what seemed miles of ice, or, if you were a first-class performer, join with Hornby in weaving patterns about an orange. One of these hard winters must have been January of 1881, when there was such a snowfall that all trains were stopped, and most country boys came back several days late.

Of course, the woes of school were as acute as the joys. There were weeks in which nothing would go right, and my tutor said, " You are a very naughty fellow." There were quarrels: for days you might not be on speaking terms with the boy you messed with. When this became known, it was the practice of other so-called friends to convey books, pictures, and ornaments from the room of each party and deposit them in that of the other. The two of you would then meet in the passage, each loaded with a cargo of the other's possessions, and with set faces would say : " I believe these things belong to you ? " and gravely exchange them ; watched with interest by the conspirators. The most serious of these feuds was occasioned by my

having placed in H. Wood's bed a dead frog :
an animal for which he had an almost
superstitious horror. (I am reminded here of a
small boy whom I visited at his private school.
He produced a box from his pocket and
showed me a live stag-beetle therein. " I'm going
to put it in my Enemy's bed," he said.) In other
cases one would become the confidant of both
parties to a quarrel, and have to do one's best to
hold the balance true and not sympathize too
much or too little with either. Besides which,
at first there were sure to be some people,
probably two or three Elections above, who took
opportunities of making life unpleasant, and were
quite cordially hated. The tongue is the most
effective weapon which is permanently at a boy's
disposal. I imagine that now, as then, all the
most rankling griefs and wounds are inflicted by
it. If someone whom you do not know says to
you in passing " You little beast " or " You great
ass," and says it with real conviction, he has
gone far to destroy your peace of mind and prejudice your outlook on your fellows for that day.
Unless, to be sure, you are of that temperament
which demands instant satisfaction at the point
of the knuckle, and also gets it. Agonies, too,
I have seen being suffered by those who stood on
the border-line between colours and no colours :
they might get their Boats or their College
Field, or they might not. Of these I was
merely a spectator—not uninterested, I hope,

when a friend was concerned, but losing no sleep.

But, after all, the most depressing periods were those in which you were expecting that delinquencies, the results of which you could bear with calmness as long as they were between you and your division master, would get round to your tutor, or to the Master in College, and form the subjects of *tête-à-tête* interviews. To have to produce a yellow ticket in pupil-room for your tutor's signature leads to all sorts of disturbing inquiries on his part ; there may even be letters to and from distressed parents, and however callous a bearing you may assume, this is not a pleasant situation. A poet has said that the thoughts of youth are long thoughts, and I believe I know what he meant. They are not long enough, however, in the sense of far-sighted, to enable a boy in trouble to look ahead : he is a mass of misery unrelieved, and sees no break in the clouds. But it is April with him, fortunately, and when the sun shows symptoms of coming out again, it will not be difficult to persuade him to sit up and partake of a little nourishment. It was a profound remark of Ecclesiastes that there does come a time when the clouds return after the rain.

Nourishment ! It played so large a part in imagination and realization that it is ungrateful not to touch upon it, though this shall be done lightly, for I cannot bring myself to write in the

horrid greedy way that even so great a man as
Thackeray condescends to, about savoury things
to eat. (I must confess, however, that I rather
enjoy reading the stuff.)

A word as to the sock-shops. I trust I shall
not be doing violence to the feelings of any
survivors if I record the curious population of
two of them. At Westbrook's, where you bought
some outlandish fruits, you met an incredibly
old and small lady in a black dress and spectacles,
and a flaxen-haired young woman whose face
seemed to have been roughly hewn—apparently
with some blunt instrument, as the police reports
say (and were saying as far back as the Cour-
voisier trial in 1840)—out of a block of wood.
Her home was obviously the forest. At Califano's
we have read in Mr. Parker's pages that it was a
perilous adventure to ask the proprietor *why
he got the sack from the Castle.* I can add a
confirmation of this. Cecil Baring, passing the
shop one day, was moved to pick a potato off a
barrow in the street and dash it against the bosom
of Califano, who was standing in his doorway
clad in spotless white. The potato smashed.
Califano instantly drew his knife and pursued
Cecil Baring along the street. He, realizing
that his life was at stake, rushed into New &
Lingwood's, and after a breathless explanation
hid himself under the counter. Califano followed,
" demanding him from all the winds," but Mrs.
Lingwood—comparable to several well-known

heroines whose names escape me for the moment —declared that no one answering to the description given, or any other, had entered the shop that morning, and C. Baring was saved.

Doubtless the proportion of our cash that we spent on sock was large ; but I can't pretend to regret it. Did I, in the eighteen halves I was at Eton, squander more than £25 in all on socking? —I don't count provisions supplied for the mess. I doubt it. Could it have been better employed ? Cries of " No ! " Regrettable orgies there were. It is still remembered that in 1862 on St. Andrew's Day, Bulteel, K.S., Keeper of the Wall, ate thirteen sausages for breakfast and lost the match by thirteen shies. There punishment followed close on the heels of crime. I have seen the Vicar of Fordingbridge eat fourteen eggs—scrambled—in Chamber tea-room : but on him no bolt fell and there is no moral. In my last halves, I and another have frequently sent out after twelve for twenty-four new halfpenny buns from Webber's, or twenty-four new rice cakes, which were entirely forgotten by Hall-time—at two. " University College has seen this," said Dr. Johnson, in reference to some terrific consumption of port achieved by him : Eton College has seen far more impressive performances in the way of eating.

Let us leave the more sordid aspects of the subject, and contemplate those which appeal to higher sentiments. A rosy light hangs about

Tea. Tea on a whole school-day in the dark
months. You might have to go out again afterwards to your tutor's for Private Business, but
that was not every night. There were two
Tea-rooms in my day : Chamber and Upper.
Both were cheerful places, but of Upper Tea-
room I have the more vivid picture in my mind.
If the mess was in funds you spent a very pleasant
half-hour or less there ; it was at least as quiet
as the parrot-house at the Zoo. I say once more
that I am not going to dilate on what we ate :
you may gain a very exact idea from G. Nugent
Bankes's two books, *A Day of My Life at Eton*
and *About Some Fellows*, which are just co-
eval with me, and (particularly the latter) are
most truthful and excellent reading. I recall,
however, that sometimes there were disappoint-
ments in the matter of bought foods. Tatham's
mess was confronted with a tin labelled *Cumber-
land Roast Chicken*, which defied all tin-openers
for a long time and was battered into a shapeless
mass. When at last an opening was effected, a
sigh of fetid air came from it, and the contents
rose in a fountain through the aperture. It was
cold sausages from a tin which may, for what
I know, nearly have ended my career in my first
half, and did succeed in keeping me in bed for
some long time. Tea in one's own room, in
Liberty or Sixth Form, was naturally an improvement on the publicity of Tea-room. What with
a fire of your own, and fags to cater for you, and

probably more elbow-room in the way of expenditure, how should you not have been happy? A College serving-man came after a while and cleared up. John Man, who left us under a cloud, supplies me with a vignette of school life. R. S. de Havilland and H. B. Smith messed together in Sixth Form Passage. De Havilland, always a sufferer from asthma, had stayed out of early school with it one winter morning. The fire was lit, the gas was on. De Havilland was sitting up in bed smoking datura tatula. H. B. Smith was seated on the bed breakfasting. What, what, would the Open Air Brigade say? We cannot wonder that John Man, coming out into the Passage after completing his work within, was heard to say " Strikes cold comin' out of Mr. dee'Avilland's room this mornin'." He was succeeded by Charley Cross, a mild man, thought by us to be mentally deficient, who lifted his feet when he walked (I quote Arthur Benson) as if they were boxes. He was not devoid of humour. One day he was at the top of a tall ladder in Weston's Yard, and Tatham, passing by, made as if to pull it away. Charley Cross looked down at him unmoved and said rather sadly: "Don't do that, Sir. Good men are scarce."

IX

I HAVE touched on a good many sides of an Eton boy's life as it was in my time, but there are several that I have only casually noticed. One of these is Chapel[1] and those whom we saw there. First, of the Provost and Fellows. In 1876 there was still a full complement of that body. Seven was the number of the Fellows. The Founder had ordained ten, but the diminution of the endowment by Edward IV had cut down the numbers, and they fluctuated for a time and finally remained at seven. Not very often were all of them to be seen at once in Chapel, for they took their turns of residence (most of them holding livings elsewhere) like Canons of a Cathedral. Dupuis (Vice-Provost), Bishop Chapman, Coleridge, Balston, Wilder, W. L. Eliot, W. A. Carter (Bursar)—these were the holders when I came. Soon Eliot died and was replaced by F. E. Durnford, hitherto Lower Master, whose right to a Fellowship on the old terms had been reserved to him by the Commissioners. He was

---

[1] What wonderful statements do get into print! I happened just now to look up Eton in Fullarton's *Gazetteer of the World*, published in the 'fifties, and I read as follows: " The Chapel, *formerly called Christopher-hall*, is an elegant Gothic structure," etc. I despair of tracing this to its source.

the last so elected. Gradually they died out.
The new " Governing Body " of elective repre-
sentatives of various bodies grew as they dwindled,
and after the death of William Carter, and in the
Statutes of 1904, the title of Provost and Fellows
became the correct one for the Governing Body.

The way in which we were made conscious of
the existence of the Fellows was by their ministra-
tions in Chapel, at the altar and in the pulpit.
I suppose I must have heard all of them preach :
" heard," though, is not the right word : I have
been aware that they were preaching. Probably
the most audible was Balston. He has come to be
rather a tragic figure to me—though I daresay I
waste my pity. What I am thinking of is that
while he was a tutor and a Head Master everybody loved and honoured him : so, too, they did in
his parish of Bakewell ; but we only sighed when
he mounted the pulpit—never thought twice
about the distinguished part he had played in the
history of Eton—and only remembered that he
appeared to have a mutton-chop bone in his throat
and said things like " To sin is wrong : you know
that : why do you do it ? " I don't think,
however, that it is fair to expect far-sighted,
thoughtful gratitude from boys. Wilder, indeed,
was an instance of one whom in his last years
the School did delight to honour : a man who
remembered the jubilee of George III, lived to
see the two jubilees of Queen Victoria, and spent
not less than £30,000 in beautifying the College

buildings. He, in fact, emerged at the last from the shadowy existence into which most of his colleagues—once such active and familiar figures —had passed. For they *were* shadows. We couldn't hear what they said : we were only sure there was too much of it : and unless we happened to be sons of old pupils or something of that kind, we never entered their houses. Nor did we feel much curiosity as to what they had been before they took their places, white-headed, skull-capped, silk-gowned, in the Chapel stalls. Only upon the stern-faced Bursar did we Collegers look with—I fear—disfavour, for we imagined that to him we owed the lateness of the date at which fires began in the Winter half, and the withholding of desired amenities—what, I cannot even conjecture now.

It is hard for me to write the words, but even Provost Goodford was to most of us as shadowy a being as the rest. He had been an admirable Head Master, and was, before and after that, an admirable man. But there it was. We called him the Cogger because his initials were C. O. G. We watched him with some amusement when—on Founder's Day and Election Monday—he brought round the grace-cup to us in Hall. We imitated (I can still do it with great accuracy, as I conceive) his rendering of the opening words of the Commination Service and the few fragments of a sermon which reached us. Thus passes the glory of the world. Doubtless the case was the same with Hawtrey before him, *mutatis mutandis*, and with Hornby after him : possibly even with Warre, though this is hard to believe ; conceivably it is the same—but no, we have reached the limit. And yet . . . there *are* boys, I know, to whom *nothing* is sacred.

The mention of the Commination Service leads me to recall points of ritual. The Provosts of Eton and King's, Goodford and Okes, were the last persons I heard read the full notice of the Communion, and the full exhortations in the Communion Service. Celebrations were then not more than monthly. It is my belief that we stood up for the *Gloria in excelsis*. I can say with certainty that that was the usage in ordinary country churches, and I cannot think why it has not subsisted. The hymn in question is no less a hymn and no more a prayer than the *Te Deum*.

On Wednesdays and Fridays our morning service consisted of a hymn and the Litany, sung. This was not a suitable service for boys : it merely meant a little folding of the hands to sleep. You wrapped your gown about your arms, your head sank into its folds, and your thoughts travelled whither they would till you became unconscious.

Saints' day services were, as I remember, the ordinary daily service *plus* the Ante-Communion. College of course wore surplices. There was an annual uncertainty on Tuesday in Whitsun week as to whether it should be surplices or gowns, and a great running to and fro on the part of those who had wrongly decided on gowns.

Confirmation took place in the Easter half. On three or four Sundays preceding it the Head Master delivered what were called Lectures on the Catechism from the pulpit at evening chapel. Hornby's were very good, and were audible. The custom was a relic of the office of Catechist, which I find beginning in 1626, when a Fellow (usually the Vice-Provost) receives £6 for the work. At that time, and until living memory, Collegers were catechised *vivâ voce* in Chapel, latterly by a Conduct: a well-known passage in a letter of Horace Walpole's refers to that rite.

On Confirmation Day itself, Collegers were obliged to attend the whole service : I forget if the obligation extended to any Oppidans. It was not a happy arrangement : the *ennui* was severe. I don't think any minor change has been more marked or more salutary than the change from Confirmation as I remember it to what I see now. Chapel is filled to overflowing by the parents and friends of the confirmands. The boys of the choirs of both Chapels attend and sing beautifully at intervals during the laying on of hands, and what used to be a weary two hours has become a memorable act of worship.

Of sermons as delivered by the Provost and Fellows I have said something. Quite often, and increasingly often in my days, preachers from the

Staff or from outside occupied the pulpit. Some were of great eminence, as Dean Stanley. Him we could not hear at our end, though we were interested more than a little by the sight of him. The only thing I do remember is that he would not leave the pulpit at the end of the service, having been, I suppose, imperfectly informed as to our ritual.

At that period there was a wide-spread belief among the preachers who came to us from outside that no sermon could be rightly preached at Eton without a reference to George Augustus Selwyn. Seldom has a great and noble memory suffered more from injudicious celebration than in his case : if I conceive of him rightly, he would have been the least patient of all listeners to what we were obliged to hear. One excellent man suffered a cruel injustice at our hands. He began a sentence with words to this effect : " Of course, when I was at Eton, and was in the Eleven and the Eight." At this, a sharp intake of the breath, almost amounting to a subdued whistle of incredulity, ran round the sacred edifice, and we decided that senile mendacity had here reached its limit. But the statement was perfectly true : he *was* one of the few people who had won that Double Blue, and anyone who wishes to be assured of the facts can see them set out in a correspondence in the *Chronicle* of a recent year.[1]

Of the Staff, I sat under Joynes, Warre, Stone,

---

[1] Viz. 1923, May 24, and following numbers.

Daman, Dalton, at least. Joynes was the most kindly listened to. His simple piety and sincerity could not be misconstrued: but he did not escape being burlesqued. He was over-fond of dealing in obvious antitheses. " Good, not bad, industrious, not idle." " I knew a boy once ; he was good, not bad, etc., etc. I used to go to his room and find him reading Good Books. None of your yellow-backed novels—*the* Book, etc., etc. *He's dead now* " (with frightful emphasis). " Before he doyed he wrote me a lettur. I'll read it to ye. It began ' Dear Mr. Joynes.' " His son Herman Joynes was a K.S. at that time and was known to us as " the Chinaman." Consequently, when his father incautiously said from the pulpit " Look at the Chinaman. He's industrious, not oidle," and the rest, we were in a position to comply at once with the preacher's injunction, and did so.

Inaudible sermons, of which, as you have gathered, there were many, inevitably led to long contemplations of the furniture and adornments of Chapel, especially the windows. Fourteen of these had been given by Wilder. (" *Has quatuordecim fenestras, septem a boreali septem ab australi huiusce ecclesiæ parte, tabellis in vitro pictis adornandas curavit. Joh. Wilder Soc.*") A great deal has been said and written about their demerits, but we found solace in them. Tatham's picturesque description of the viands provided for Belshazzar's feast sticks in my mind : according

to him they consisted of " three toads in a plate
and a bath-can of lemonade." Isaac's dressing-
gown was also popular, and the cloud of smoke,
apparently cut from a solid mass of mutton-fat,
which is to be seen in the Tabernacle. No, they
are not good. Even the three eastern windows,
designed by Willement, who was a pioneer in his
day, suffer from the thinness of the material,
and the drawing is open to criticism. " What a
pore face that is, if we may say so," was the
constant remark of old Burgess, the Chapel clerk,
when he showed visitors round, and pointed to the
principal scene in the east window. By dint of
darkening with paint and insertion of wooden
cross-bars that east window has been made far
less garish. The north and south windows in the
eastern bay are as they were : bad as the colour is,
the character of the design reproduces with a good
deal of success the " feel " of the German glass
of the early sixteenth century.

I have several times been pleasantly surprised
by boys telling me that the window they like best
is the one at the west end above the organ. It is
a mere kaleidoscope without any pictures, but
in it are the only surviving relics of the old glass,
collected and arranged there at the expense of
Mr. Coleridge, the Fellow. The instinct of the
boys is right, therefore : they can recognize a
good colour when they see it, and the blue is
particularly good.

I am tempted, having mentioned these relics,

to dilate for a little on the general question of our old glass. Everybody knows that our sister College of King's has been allowed to keep its splendid equipment of glass complete; and *à propos* of that, I have often been asked what Eton used to possess in that line. It is very difficult to say. I think we may be pretty confident that our windows were never filled like those at King's with a series of pictures conceived on a definite plan. We do know this much : in the old parish church, which stood south of the churchyard and served for many years as the College church, there was a set of prophets and apostles in the windows. These may or may not have been moved to the new church. In the new church there was certainly a picture of the Annunciation in the east window, for the College accounts tell of money paid for mending the lily-pot. (Need I explain that the lily-pot is the indispensable adjunct to the Annunciation—standing between Gabriel and the Virgin ?) In view of the fact that the Chapel is dedicated to the Assumption of the Virgin, I cannot doubt that this scene also figured conspicuously in the east window. The accounts tell us another interesting thing which has not been enphasized—if recorded at all—by our historians. In the first quarter of the sixteenth century the glazier regularly employed on the Chapel windows was Galen Hoone. This man, a Fleming resident in London, was the maker of the greater part of the King's College windows ; he was the official glazier to the King, succeeding Barnard Flower. Thus there is reason to suppose that our Chapel possessed some windows at least of work similar to that at King's. To Galen Hoone I attribute the medallions (sadly broken), illustrating various branches of learning, which are still to be seen in the windows of Election Hall. I have described them in detail in *Etoniana*. The only place where bits of the Chapel glass are rumoured to exist is at our church of Worplesdon in Surrey. I have examined the fragments, but do not find them very helpful. Some names of female saints can be read, *e.g.* St. Christina. But the scale of these is not large enough to allow of their having been placed in the upper windows of the Chapel. In short, there is no certainty that all our windows contained painted glass. Nor can the fate of those that did be clearly made out. There is no record of systematic destruction : there *is* record of constant mending, in some years very extensive. Once, in 1616, payment is made for coloured glass to supply defects in the east window. I must suppose that the pictures gradually dropped to pieces and were replaced by plain glass. Scattered bits no doubt survived in the tracery lights and the tops of the larger lights : enough to fill the window which started this discussion.

It is a dreadful temptation, now that I have broached antiquarian matters, to go on and discóurse about the wall-paintings, but I will confine myself to what I knew of them as a boy. Maxwell-Lyte's *History* (1875) was the first source of information. From that I learnt of the existence of the paintings behind the stalls and was consumed with desire to see them. Next, when I obtained access to the College Library, I ferreted out the portfolio of Essex's drawings of them which were made in 1847. Then, in 1881-2, Street was employed to erect a new organ screen of stone, and the stalls at the west end were temporarily removed. Here was a chance of seeing something, and I did see the two figures of female saints which terminate the series on the north and south walls. Alas! those months were the last of Street's life. He was ill, and unable personally to supervise the work going on in Chapel. Otherwise he, who at the time of the discovery of the paintings had been loudest in their praise, would undoubtedly have seen to it that no part of them should suffer injury at his hands. As it was, his workmen built the ends of his screen right into the paintings, and severely injured St. Sidwell and St. Winifred. The stonework was cut away from them in 1924, but they are in a sad state. For the rest, I will only repeat a statement I have often made of late, that in these paintings Eton possesses a treasure which is, honestly, unrivalled in this country and in France. You must go as far as Italy (or almost as far: we must not forget Avignon) before you can find wall-paintings of equal importance and beauty.

Another relic of ancient times used to excite my interest. In the ante-chapel are two curious buttresses flanking the arch into the choir. They are surmounted by two stone statues, the only mediaeval images that remain in the building : they stand too high up to be readily got at by iconoclasts. You may see them in Ackermann's print of about 1811. One is very obviously St. George. The other is a king, whom I always supposed to be either Edward the Confessor or Henry VI. Only in this present summer have I succeeded in getting photographs made of them, by help of a scaffolding erected for the cleaning of the organ. I now see that the king is St. Edmund the Martyr, for he holds two arrows. They are works of very considerable merit.

Yet another relic—now lost—shall be recorded, and then I will drop antiquarian matters for the moment. Penetrating one day (in my last year) into the disused brewhouse, we found some very richly carved fragments of stone, with foliage beautifully under-cut. These had come from the pinnacles of the Chapel, which were reconstructed in the early seventies. Following their common practice, the seventeenth or eighteenth century repairers of those pinnacles had used up any convenient-sized bits of stuff and made them up with cement to the required form. The carvings in question were pieces of the mediaeval reredos at the east end. Between 1882 and 1918 they have been lost sight of. Possibly they may still turn up in somebody's rockery.

The length of my disquisition on Chapel services, coupled with my former discourse on the music, gives, I hope, the impression, which is the true one, that they interested us very much. But we should not have been human boys if we had not been *specially* interested in anything that went wrong in the course of them. Now that I am ultimately responsible for the proper performance of them, and for the avoidance of mistakes, a *contretemps* causes me acute pain. It was not so between 1876 and 1882. To us, horribly watchful, it was pure joy when an inadvertent preacher left his seat to go to the pulpit without waiting for Holderness the verger to conduct him, and when Holderness, unwisely insistent on his duty, would follow him shakily— for he was old—and vainly dodge and tack to see if by chance he could get in front of the preacher. In such cases no facilities were given by the boys who occupied the knifeboard. The gangway was made narrower than usual, not broader. Boys are not always kind.

Again, we were not embarrassed, in dutiful sympathy with the Provost, but pleased, when one day, through some misunderstanding, neither of the two Conducts turned up at morning Chapel, and after a wait of some minutes one of the

Fellows (Eliot, I think) was hustled into a surplice and hood, and, smiling shyly, proceeded to do the best he could. Nor when Mr. Vidal the Conduct (who was subject to lapses of memory : Errington was not) would forget that it was a Litany morning and begin Matins : then, recollecting himself, would say audibly " No, I don't mean that : Hymn 281," or *vice versa*. Nor on one terrible Sunday morning when the service was earlier than usual and Barnby failed to appear. The choir were therefore unaccompanied and had not expected to be : the *Venite* was sung to the treble of one chant and bass of another. The Psalms were given out. " The third morning of the month : Psalm xv." Orlando Christian, the bass of the Decani side, sang three verses by himself ; his too timid colleagues did nothing. It was a gallant effort, but he could not keep it up. There was a silence. Then the Conduct took command and the psalms were read. By the time the *Te Deum* was reached, Barnby had been roused and conveyed to the organ loft—in a nightgown and slippers, *we* said. I believe that on this occasion we did sympathize with Orlando Christian, at least : an absolute *fiasco* is not really relished even by boys. They look down their noses, just like human beings, if the agony is at all protracted.

Before I finally leave the subject of Chapel, I must be allowed a word about the Bells, even if my promise not to be antiquarian again just yet has to be broken. All School-notices about Chapel services say " Bells begin at so-and-so." There is but one bell used. The other, the knell bell, is reserved for funerals. But I hope and believe that the expression is a real survival of the time when we had five bells, hung in a timber campanile in the churchyard. The Puritans dismantled them and they were laid up at the " upper " (*i.e.* east) end of the church. In 1766 (I think) they were sold for old metal. (At King's, exactly the same thing happened to *their* peal of five bells.) Chapel bell or bells mean a great deal to the boys. Chapel is one of the things you must *not* be late for. The tolling begins at ten minutes before the service and used to go on till the proper minute and then give three or four quick beats and cease as the organ sounded and the procession of Sixth Form got under way. Nowadays there is an interval of three or four minutes' silence on the part of the bell, during which Chapel fills : but there is still the quickened beat at the end— a dreadful sound to some wretched boy who finds himself on Barnes Pool Bridge or somewhere down Keate's Lane. It is still the subject of nightmares with me : I am at the further end of College, looking feverishly for my surplice, and I hear the Bell say " bang-bang-bang," and despair fills my breast. And still, even in waking hours, when something has prevented me from being present, I do not feel quite comfortable when I hear the final beats, and the swell of the organ coming across Schoolyard.

There must be a great many people about the world to whom Chapel is on the whole the best beloved Church. Like me they greet with a quite peculiar thrill the glimpse of the gold vanes on the eastern cupolas, which may just be seen by those who are whirling down to the West in an express train. Blest is the man (probably Mr. Matthew Banks, the King's carpenter) who about the year 1690 designed those cupolas and vanes, surmounted by golden lilies. No more thoroughly incongruous, no more completely successful addition to a Gothic building was ever made. It is to them that I would point if someone asked me to show him the most significant, the best-remembered feature of Eton.

Return we to the impressions and events of the latter end of my school life.

X

THERE were literary aspirations, of course: most premature. Ephemerals were not so common then as now, when their object is too often merely "profitable pecuniary emolument." The *Eton Rambler*, however, was started in College about 1880, and ran through two or three numbers: my own contributions to it I cannot now look at with patience. A communication to the *Academy* there was, too, about a fragment of a MS. Latin Plutarch I had found in a binding in the library at Bury St. Edmund's. I suppose it now to have been from a fifteenth century humanist version: at the time I believed it to be much older. In my last year I was more reputably employed, as editor of the *Chronicle*, my colleague being St. Clair Donaldson. The *Chronicle* was then a fortnightly: the editorial wage was at the rate of 15s. per number for each editor. Some devastating attempts at humour are to be found—but I hope no one will look for them—in my numbers. The principal debt I owe to my one period of journalistic work is that it brought me into close touch with my fellow editor—now Bishop of Salisbury.

. . . .

The tone of these recollections has been, and
I foresee will be, largely rather frivolous. I have
designedly kept out of them my home ties, and
the expression of emotions with which I may be
reasonably believed to be familiar. But I do not
see how I can leave unmentioned an event
which concerned the deeper things of life. On
May 24, 1882, Seton Donaldson—then Donaldson *mi.*—was drowned near Sandbank. On him
many bright hopes and great affection were
centred, for he was a boy of high character and
promise : it is curious to reflect that, well as I
knew his elder brothers, the master, Stuart,
and the boy, St. Clair, I had never spoken to
him. In the weeks that followed that tragedy I
saw much of the brothers, of their mother and
their home. The friendship, which had begun
lightly and casually, was deepened and solidi-
fied, to my great gain. The name of Seton
Donaldson remains among the sacred things.

" So Lycidas sunk low, but mounted high,
   Through the dear might of Him that walked the waves."

That was his epitaph in our minds.

.   .   .   .

Apart from that shadow, the last summer
half—indeed, the whole of the last three halves—
seem to me invested with an air of glory. School
matters had gone very well. In January I got
my Scholarship at King's, in March the Newcastle. My circle was not small, inside College

or outside. The kindnesses one received from Masters were numberless, and I was charging about into literature ancient and modern like a bull in a china shop. Memory also presents the summer as having been extremely fine and hot. Furthermore, I was of an age to be conscious that I was very happy : for, a day or two before I left Eton for Camp, my twentieth birthday came round ! Impossible now, but not without precedent then.

So, in the first days of August 1882, I ceased to be an Eton boy.

.   .   .   .

I am now writing on the first day of a Michaelmas half, forty-three years later. To-day I admitted five new Collegers, thereby marking for them probably the most important stage that they will arrive at till they are married or die. After that I stood at the window of Lupton's Tower and watched, as I often watch, the gathering of the School for Absence. Assault and battery is committed with umbrellas—for it is raining— boys play Fives with a football against Chapel wall. Saving their reverences, one cannot but be reminded of kittens and puppies : the maturer and nobler animals will be in evidence later in the week, for they have not all come back yet. New boys stand aloof, not venturing on any liberties. It is of them that I naturally think most when, returning to these reminiscences, I reflect how the wheel has come full circle, and here I sit writing in the Provost's Lodge, in a room not many feet distant from those which I used to inhabit. What are the new lot going to make of it ? I only hope that when they come to the day of leaving, and march off, as most of them will, past Upper School and Chapel towards the station on their way to Camp, they will be carrying with them a treasure of memories as precious and enduring as I did when I'went by that road.

XI

SINCE then I am thankful to say I have never lost touch with Eton. But the venue has now to be changed, and we concentrate upon King's.

I believe it is necessary to remind you of what King's had been, and how it was changing. Under the Founder's Statutes, which remained in force until the First University Commission of 1855, it was a society of a Provost and seventy persons. How recruited ? Every year towards the end of July the Provost of King's and two Fellows selected for the purpose and known as Posers (Opposers, Apposiers, in the old Accounts) came to Eton and held an examination to elect Scholars of King's from among the Collegers. There was great feasting and great doings among the authorities during these days. Considerable payments for wine at Election occur yearly in the accounts : tenants and neighbours sent game : hangings, rushes, sometimes flowers, were hired and bought for the Posers' rooms. Tobacco and pipes appear in the middle of the seventeenth century. Most of the older books of Eton reminiscences tell in detail of the ceremonies that had to be performed. The only relics of them that survived into my time were the half-chicken apiece and the grace-cup which we had in Hall on Election Monday. I will just add (for I do not remember to have seen it in the books), on the authority of my father, that on Election Monday, and then only, the Bible on the iron desk by the High Table was used. The chapter uniformly read, by a Scholar, was Job xxv, which has but six verses. The Bible (a Latin Vulgate) is still in the College safe.

The examination of Scholars at Election had come to be purely formal. As far as I can tell, from the moment you entered College your seniority was fixed, and it would have been considered an outrage to disturb the order. As time went on it became clearer whether you could " get King's " or not; but there was still an element of uncertainty, for there might be no vacancy made in the number of seventy who constituted King's. The lists in fact show that in some years there *was* none, in others only one or two. Vacancies were made by death, marriage, acceptance of a living, or of course resignation from any other cause. The number of Collegers called up from Eton naturally tallied with the number of vacancies.

Once a Scholar of King's, you proceeded *without examination* to your Bachelor's Degree and to your Fellowship, and there you were, barring the acts or accidents I have mentioned, for life.

These arrangements were taken over bodily

from the Winchester and New College Statutes by our Founder. What the outcome of them had been in comparatively modern times you may see portrayed in a very lively way by an ancient Mr. Tucker, the last survivor of the untouched system. He had published an equally interesting book, *Eton of Old : or Eighty Years Since* (1892), on the strength of which Oscar Browning, very wisely, asked him to write down his memories of King's. He did so, and some few typewritten copies of his MS. were made, of which I own one. The whole has now been printed by our admirable Eton historiographer, Mr. R. A. Austen Leigh, in his magazine *Etoniana*.

Mr. Tucker gives, as I said, lively details of daily life. There is another monument of old King's called the Scholar's Book, which was circulated in manuscript and contained a record of the formal usages which had to be complied with. I possess a copy of this "To be kept by the Senior Scholar for the time being." I daresay it represents the conditions prevalent about 1790 : 1777 is the latest date mentioned in the text. I am tempted to quote a few paragraphs, for I believe they have never seen the light. The text begins with :

"NEW SCHOLAR'S ADMISSION.

" A Scholar must, on pain of losing his right, be here within twenty days after regular notice has been given him by the Provost of Eton and the (Head) Master. The Scholar who expects him for his chamber-fellow must visit the Provost or in his absence the Vice-Provost with an Epistle."

(This business of " visiting " the authorities crops up over and over again : one gets the impression that it might have consumed no small part of the day.)

" The junior Scholar fetches the Freshman to College, sends for the Tailor to provide a gown and cap, carries him soon to the Provost with his letter " (that is, the credential from the Provost of Eton, which is still issued) " or in his absence to the Vice-Provost, takes care of him till he is admitted, directs him to stand in Stain-coat-hole before grace " (this Staincoat or Stangate hole was under the screens at the entrance to Hall) " and under the organ loft at Chapel : asks the time of his admission, sees that he reads the admission statutes : provides Greek Testament and the Public Notary at the time of admission : makes him stand under the bell, or Provost's Lodge, till called in " (this is obscure).

" After admission the Freshman is placed in a chamber by the Provost, the Vice-Provost attending, or by the Vice-Provost, a Dean attending. During his Freshmanship " (a week) " he goes not without his chamber-fellow, caps the Courts and Chapel, goes to Hall and Chapel at the first ringing of the bell : stands bare in the Hall at the upper end of the Scholars' table : reads Greek Testament when he sits down to one of the senior Scholars till taken off by the Steward or other graduate Fellows *his verbis* ' *Parce tyroni* ' : has verses before him all the canon hours : writes the admission statutes or senior Scholar's book " (the document before us) " the week of his Freshmanship.

" Mem.   Canon hours begin after Chapel in the morning " (which I think was at 7) " and last till our Clock strikes 8.   In the evening begin at 8 and last till 9.   The junior or Nib of each chamber must keep the door shut all canon hours on his peril, nor admit of any stranger, nor be without tinder-box and other necessaries.   The Scholars   visit   the   Pro :,   V.-Pro :,   Deans " (there were three of these) " and Lecturers for going out of College (except to St. Mary's or the Schools) with verses at eight or afterwards till they find them.   After sitting bare the Scholars go to their chambers for an hour and then visit. Scholars cap even junior Fellows in the Court: they walk not in the Chapel yard walk : they strike " (that is, take off their caps to) " Masters of Arts in Chapel yard and Couches" (unknown, this) " except   when   a   stranger   is   between." (And many other suchlike things they do.)

" A Freshman is in all customs and cere-monies of the College to be instructed by the senior Scholar and his chum, attending him in and out of his chamber during his Freshmanship week, lest he ignorantly alone should commit absurdities.   He is to visit the Pr., V.Pr., Deans, and Lecturers after a week or ten days' Fresh-manship, to be out thereof, *his verbis*, ' *oro me hoc tyrocinio liberes.*' "

Fortunately for everyone concerned there were but very few Freshmen undergoing this penance

at any one moment. We will proceed a little
further.

"CUSTOMS TO BE OBSERVED BY THE SCHOLAR.

" The 2 senior Scholars are to visit the Pro :,
V. Pro :, Deans and Lecturers for Non-
Terms " (*i.e.* holidays, remission of lectures and
the like) " and Dors " (*i.e.* long lies in the
morning).

" There are four solemn beavers in the year,
for the remembrance of which there is a false
verse :

"Andreas, Thomas, Sanctorum, Nativitasque."

(false enough, in all conscience) " on the eves
whereof the Fellows and Scholars meet at six
o'clock in the Hall, when each having a Q "
(cue, it is still called, in the case of audit ale) " of
Bread and Beer, they are to drink Charity to
each other ; on which eves, as also on the said
fastnights, the Scholars keep canon hour in
Hall, and call them Crambo nights, from an
old custom of playing then at Crambo."

After this follows the

"SCHOLARS' CALENDAR.

" Jan. 6th. The senior Scholar visits after
supper for a Dor next morning.

" 7th. They visit again for a Dor the 8th in
memoriam Doctoris Cowell, because then and
never else he overslept himself and missed early
prayers." (This is Dr. Cowell, the not unknown
author of the *Interpreter*.)

The number of holidays (or days in which term

is out) is not inconsiderable : five days before and five days after the Purification : likewise before and after Ash Wednesday: 15 days before Easter : three days before Whitsuntide and all Whitsun week: ten full days before St. John Baptist—" and it continues out for good and all ": five days before and after 5 November : Founder's Day and all the 12 days (of Christmas).

The rest of the book is interesting enough, but it is chiefly concerned with the taking of degrees. What I have quoted shows an odd mixture of mediaeval formalism and, I should say, slackness. They got the boys up early and harried them at certain times of the day, and for the rest did not trouble themselves much with anything you could call education.

This old system was fundamentally changed by the Commission. The Statutes of 1861—the outcome of their labours—opened the College to non-Etonians, and ordained that there should be 24 Eton and 24 open scholarships, and 46 Fellows. The next Commission, resulting in the Statutes of 1882, under which we lived, did not alter this provision, but made other changes, of which the most prolific in results (naturally, perhaps) was that which permitted the Fellows to marry, and also made Fellowships terminable after six years unless the holder was doing work for the College or held certain University offices.

XII

I THINK this glimpse into statutes will suffice to explain the character of the Society into which I entered in 1882. It was composed of several strata. There was the Provost, Okes, who had been summoned from the post of Lower Master at Eton in 1850 ; and with him were perhaps fifteen Fellows under the Founder's Statutes, a majority of whom were non-residents and seldom seen by us. This was the first stratum. The next consisted of the Fellows elected under the Statutes of 1861. Among these were some non-Etonians. Lastly there were the B.A.'s (some of whom were looking to be made Fellows under the new Statutes of 1882), the Scholars, and other undergraduates. My year consisted of fifteen, of whom I was the only Etonian: the year before was just twice as large and had four Etonians : the preceding one was of twenty-two, with three Etonians. The total of undergraduates, therefore, in residence was sixty-seven.

For us the *ancien régime* was represented by the Provost and about seven senior Fellows who were pretty constantly in residence. They were a remarkable body. I think I must try to sketch them, some more, some less fully.

Provost Okes had been enthroned in the Lodge, as I said, since 1850, and was now nearly eighty-five and rather infirm. Only once or twice did he officiate in Chapel in my first term : he either read the Ante-Communion Service or celebrated. His voice was strong as ever, and perfectly audible in that difficult building. For some time after that he continued to attend Chapel, but could not manage the walk to the east end. It may be supposed, therefore, that we did not see very much of him. He admitted us as Scholars in the Lodge. A shortish, rather thick-set man, with white hair, and marked features which Herkomer's picture of him renders very faithfully, not missing the magpie-like expression, he sat in a chair of state enveloped in voluminous black : a red footstool was before him upon which we were to kneel in turn. Behind him stood Vice-Provost Austen Leigh and some other dark forms of Officers and Fellows. He said with great deliberation : " I shall read you a short declaration in Latin, and when I have read it, I shall expect you to answer ' Promittimus.' The declaration is this : ' Promittitisne vos omnia Statoota vos concernentia observatooros ? ' " (there may have been a little more). We all said timidly, " Promittimus," but no notice was taken. " Now I shall read the declaration : ' Promittitisne, etc.' " We all said, somewhat louder, " Promittimus." " Now I expect you to answer ' Promittimus.' " We, louder still,

" Promittimus." " I didn't hear that gentleman " (pointing) " say ' Promittimus.' " Upon
which I imagine we all said it again and were
eventually admitted, the Provost beginning the
formula with " Eego Ricardus Okes."

Only two or three personal interviews with him
do I remember, but one of them I am bound in
piety to record, for it was the outcome of his
real kindness. He had known my father, who
was a Fellow of King's, and it had come to his
ears that I, ever unwilling to rise from my bed,
had finally been gated for persistence in this
evil-doing. So he sent for me and said, " When
I was your age I used to get up at five o'clock
every morning and make myself a cup of cocoa
and do a couple of hours' work before Chapel.
Now couldn't you resolve to do something of
the same kind ? I'm sure you would find it a
great help." I was very much touched by his
taking this trouble over me : it was a most
unusual thing for him to do—unprecedented, as
far as I could discover. I have no doubt I
said that I should find it quite easy to *resolve*
to follow his advice : I hope I did so resolve.
What came of that could at one time have been
ascertained from the College gate-bills : but since
these are not stored in the University Library, as,
I gather, those of Oxford Colleges are in the
Bodleian, and I am not going to give it away,
nobody will ever be quite sure.

I have first-hand testimony to a story about

Okes which seems to me alike noteworthy and creditable to him. A small relative—say a great-nephew—was on a visit at the Lodge, and by invitation sitting reading his book in the Provost's study. A servant entered with a card : " A gentleman to see you, Sir." The Provost read the card and said, " Tell the gentleman that the Provost is not prepared to see him." After some minutes the card is handed to the small boy : " Read me what is written on that card." " The Lord Chief Justice of England." " And what sort of man do you think the Lord Chief Justice of England would be ? " All this with great deliberation. The boy, a good deal at a loss, eventually says, " A very clever man." " Yes : he is a very Clever man, but not at all a Good man. And that is the reason why you heard me say that I am not prepared to see him."

Next in seniority to the Provost was, I suppose, Andrew Long, an occasional resident and formerly Vice-Provost, who occupied rooms in Wilkins's Building, on the first floor, looking out on Chapel. I never spoke to him or heard him say anything. Reports were current that when he was not at King's he lived at the Langham Hotel. He was believed to have Taste, was a member of the Fitzwilliam Museum Syndicate, and had a painting of Chapel, unfinished, on an easel in his rooms to which he used to add a touch every now and then. Also a wen on his head, which was supposed to have assumed a separate existence and to disturb him very much by talking in the small hours. How wanting in respect are the young!

Henry Bradshaw has, as he deserves, a whole volume to himself, and that an admirable one, the Memoir by Prothero—something of a classic, I think, among biographies of scholars. Bradshaw's person was massive, his carriage stately, his face calm and noble. You felt there was nothing little about him, and the reverence and love he inspired needed no explanation. It extended to every grade and age.

Would that I had made a practice of going oftener to his rooms than I did! I think I was deterred by so seldom getting at Bradshaw himself. All sorts of dons and undergraduates might be there : some of them, like Chawner, simply sat there whole evenings and said nothing at all : others monopolised Bradshaw : whereat, as I was bursting with questions I wanted to ask him, I was discontented. It did sometimes happen, though, that one stayed late and got him almost alone. That was delightful. Two little characteristic things I will put down : one shows his impish way of disconcerting you. I had made some remark involving the word *calibre*. " Oh! you pronounce it caleeber, do you?" says Bradshaw. " How nithe!" " How ought you to pronounce it?" says I, with a pang of doubt. " Oh, *I* don't know " (with a great assumption of humility), is the only answer I can extract. The other is a curious habit of his, a liking for having the palms of his hands tickled (it would have been maddening to me) : I remember sitting doing this for quite a long time one night to one hand, while somebody else attended to the other, and Bradshaw sat and purred.

Bradshaw, let me note, was the only man I ever saw who wore, instead of the M.A. hood lined with white, the plain black hood of the non-regent M.A. Non-regents were the senior M.A.'s who were no longer under the obligation to lecture ; in old times they constituted a separate House in the Senate—the Black-hood House. Now the hood in question is reserved to Bachelors of Divinity, and all distinction between regents and non-regents is wiped out. He once told me a piece of old King's lore which I have not seen in print. It was the custom, when a celebration of the Holy Communion impended, for the Chapel Clerk to go round to all the senior Fellows, laymen and clerics alike, and ask them if they wished to celebrate. It is not known what would have happened had a layman answered in the affirmative. What curious things did he not know ? It was he who told me of the devotion of King Henry VII for St. Armagilus or Armel. In some sea-peril off the Breton coast the King, then Duke of Richmond (I imagine), had been told to invoke St. Armel, and had been preserved. Hence the image of the saint in

Henry VII's Chapel and elsewhere, and the occurrence of St. Armel in many prayer-books of the time. He it was also who gave me a name for that curious repetition of the first word of an antiphon which is regularly found in the Roman service-books. In Spain, at any rate, it appears to have been called the *pressa*.

I was not in Cambridge on that day in early February 1886 when he was found sitting at his table dead : but I went up for a Sunday before the funeral, at which I could not be present, and surely never was a society so broken with grief on a like occasion as that which I found at King's and Trinity. *Unice doctus, unice desideratus*, was the best phrase I could devise for his epitaph. It is true as far as it goes ; but no mere phrases could do justice to the memory of Bradshaw. Beyond the personal influence which he exercised (and I have never seen anything more marked ; it extended to forming the handwriting of his disciples) there was one great service which he rendered to knowledge. He taught that the same methods of exactness and the same love of truth should be the rule for students of bibliography and of art which the great men of his generation were applying to natural science.

Fred Whitting (he alone of his clan kept the old pronunciation of the name, Whiting) is to be thought of next. Earlier generations knew him best as Bursar. When Augustus Austen

Leigh became Provost in 1889, Fred became Vice-Provost, and so continued till his death in 1911. In those years the expression " the V.P." conveyed to all our minds the picture of him. It was by no means that of the conventional don. Fred was the most genial of country squires in dress and bearing. A cake hat (by which I mean a billy-cock with a flat top), a tailless coat, black on Sundays, on ordinary days of rather rough tweed, trousers inclining to the peg-top form with pockets in front, low stick-up shirt collars with a wide gap, and often—though scrupulously clean—worn down to the underlying fabric and serrated all along the edge—that was the familiar garb. His hair was growing grey, and he had a moustache and short beard. The whole outward man is splendidly given in the portrait of him by Charles Furse which hangs in our Hall : and a great deal of the inner man too, for no one can look at the picture without thinking " What a delightful man to know ! " What cannot, of course, be guessed at is his voice and manner. He had, as people say, no roof to his mouth, and to the unaccustomed he appeared to be speaking in an unknown tongue. Amiable strangers confronted with him were sure of his kindly intentions : but though he took a great deal of trouble to make himself intelligible, their answers to his inquiries were apt to be very wide of the mark. To us who lived with him it was all plain sailing. No more inspiriting sound could welcome you back to College than the trumpetings of Fred Whitting across the court, conveying an instant invitation to whatever meal might be in the offing. I have never known anybody at once more radiantly jovial and more simply good.

Coming down from his rooms at the top of Gibbs's Building, he would stroll into an undergraduate's rooms at the bottom, pick up a copy of verses, read out a line or two, and then say with conviction : " What a clever feller you are ! " If you did him the least service, it was always : " What a good feller you are ! " After a lacerating encounter at a College meeting,. he would stroke his beard and say, " Funny feller, Browning," or " Pore old Johnny Nixon ! " instead of an invective. His speech was racy and unconventional : I wish I remembered more of it accurately. " Regular three-decker," used to be his description of a stately and voluminous matron. " A very fancy lady," of one slighter and smarter. But here are some sayings which I treasure more. We have an annual sermon before the University on Lady Day in King's Chapel. One year, as he and I came out, he said to me, " I *like* a little Mariolatry. I should like to preach on the 25th of March. I should take for my text : ' Blessed art thou among women,' and give her a pat on the back." The year after, on the same day, we met at lunch. Fred was slightly pensive, then gave a short laugh, and

said, more or less to himself : " The Virgin
Mary ! She *was* a stunner ! " These things
were said with the utmost sincerity, of course,
or I should not put them down : as it was, they
were delightful ; and I couldn't help contrasting
them in my mind with what I remember reading
of—I think De Lisle—one of the early Tractar-
ians, who at Oxford " could not refrain from
bursting into tears at the mere mention of the
name of the dear Mother of Christ."

Another utterance of Fred's concerned theo-
logy. He went to stay with Herbert Ryle, then
Bishop of Winchester, at Farnham, the Arch-
bishop of Canterbury being there too. When he
came back he told me : " After breakfast they
were going off together to Ryle's study and I
said to 'em, ' I know what you two fellers are
after : you're going to try and patch up the
Athanasian Creed. You'd much better let it
alone : you won't do any good with it.' "

He must have been a sort of idol to the Choristers. Yearly on Founder's Day (6th December),
when they came and sang in Hall after our
feast, he had a great tea for them in his rooms,
and there they spent the time until they
were wanted in Hall. Among the things he
provided for their amusement was always a
roulette-board ! Whether this led to heavy
play I don't know. There was also a concertina,
which had been a fashionable instrument in his
youth. He left them in his will an annual

12

half-crown apiece, to be distributed at Christmas time.

When new University Statutes came in and a Financial Board was set up, Fred was made Secretary thereof—an indication of the respect with which his business abilities were generally regarded. He carried into that stern office the qualities which endeared him to us in King's. It seemed, as people said, to be a real pleasure to him to draw you a cheque : sonorous cries of welcome greeted you when you opened his door. Needless to say, the University loved him as his College did. On the College estates, too, though I never went circuit till after he had ceased to be Bursar, the older tenants were always enquiring after him with the greatest solicitude.

It was he who accompanied me to Lincoln when I went to be admitted Provost by our Visitor, Bishop King. I thought I should not often see two more attractive types of goodness in the same room.

He was rather hard of hearing in his last years, and under doctor's orders moved his rooms from the top of the staircase to the ground floor. In the Christmas vacation after that he went to town, partly, if I remember right, to see the grave of one of the Dawnays, whose private tutor he had been at Eton, and who had recently died. On the morning of New Year's Day, 1911, which was a Sunday, he came down into

the smoking-room of his Club, where he was
staying, just before setting off for Church—his
prayer-book in his pocket—and fell down dead.
In loco pascuae ibi collocavit me is written on
his brass.

Augustus Austen Leigh, Vice-Provost and
Dean when I came up, and later on Provost, is
the subject of a memoir by his brother Willy,
in which the story of his untiring work for
King's, which he helped so much to pilot
through the period of reform, is well and fully
told. An extraordinarily good and just man was
Augustus Leigh: devoted to duty, almost distress-
ingly modest, but completely firm when he had
made up his mind what was right. Respect was
his from everyone he had to do with, and if his
temperament would have allowed it, a warm affection. As it was, even of his contemporaries no
one could say that he knew Augustus intimately.
But the family circle of the Austen Leighs
could tell a different story: there, I think, the
reserve must have melted away: the brothers
and sisters were exceedingly fond and proud
of one another. I must not give the impression
that Augustus was cold, or an uneasy companion.
He was not: but I did feel that there was
something to be penetrated, and I never knew
anyone in the College who could be said to have
penetrated it.

Beautifully written letters used to come to me
in too many weeks of my undergraduate days:

" letters of regret " that I had not fulfilled the
alternative duties of going to Chapel or " signing
in," at 8 a.m.   Sometimes the series culminated in
the way I have mentioned.   Let it not be
thought that I was the only recipient.   A batch
of these Hugessen collected (many, no doubt,
addressed to himself) and put into a neat calf-
binding with the title " Letters of a Vice-Provost."   The proper form in which to answer
these is curious to remember.   The undergraduate did not write " Dear Mr. Vice-Provost "
or " Dear Sir," but " Dear Austen Leigh."   It
was a survival of the time when the scholar had
very likely been the fag of the don, in College—
when, at least, all had been Eton K.S.'s.   Naturally it died, as the proportion of non-Etonians
grew.   Apart from the early-rising problem, I
don't think the Vice-Provost had many disciplinary difficulties.   Most of his tribulations must
have been undergone at College meetings, whereof it will soon be inevitable to speak.   He was
on the best of terms with us, and, like Fred
Whitting, indefatigably kind to the Choristers.

This may be a proper place to insert a legend,
due, I believe, in all its parts, to the inventive-
ness of the Right Hon. W. C. Bridgeman, the
object of which was to illustrate in part the
mutual attachment of the Austen Leigh brothers,
but still more the waywardness or independence
of Edward Austen Leigh.   The whole tribe is
supposed to be assembled at his moor in Scotland,

and Augustus has sallied forth to fish and has brought home a small salmon. Willy is the first to greet him, and ejaculates, "Augustus! What a magnificent Fish is this that you have caught!" Then, speeding off, summons successively Cholmeley, Spencer, Charles, Arthur, saying to each, " Come and see the magnificent Fish that Augustus has caught," to which, after due inspection, each replies, " Yes, Augustus, this is indeed a magnificent Fish that you have caught." Finally Edward is led in, with the same exhortation. He, after regarding the Fish with some disfavour, says with extreme nicety of enunciation, " Well, Augustus, that may be your idea of a magnificent Fish. All that I can say is, that whenever I capture a fish of those dimensions, I invariably return it tew the water."

No young person so prejudiced (if you like) in favour of Eton—I would rather say, no one so grateful to Eton—as I was, could judge at all fairly of Oscar Browning : for it was his practice to take the Eton Freshman out for a walk, and, in the intervals of bumping heavily against him, pour out abuse and disparagements of Eton, and extol the day-school and its least superficially attractive products, in a way which robbed one of all desire to know the rights of the matter. Never was there a worse advocate, never one more completely satisfied of his own competence.

Such a beginning was not going to conciliate

affection. I did learn to admire O.B.[1] for many things : for the kindnesses he did to people who could make no return, for his abilities, which sometimes reminded one of genius, for his big ideas. *But*—the but is very large. I owe to him (and I can't exclude Nixon from this indictment) a profound distaste for anything in the nature of a business meeting. Oh, the prolixity, the quarrelsomeness, the relentless plying of the grindstone for his own particular axe ! And I also owe him the pernicious distaste for theorists, especially educational theorists, which I can never hope to unlearn.

But here I am more concerned with the first years. O.B.'s unremitting abuse of Eton alienated us, and nothing after that could make us perfectly easy with him. Eton, O.B. was sure, had treated *him* very badly, and therefore it must be a very bad place. *We* didn't care what had happened to him seven years before—who would ?—and we knew that Eton had given us a vast deal of what we prized most. We were much fonder of Hornby, who had dismissed him, than we were of O.B., and to hear both Eton and Hornby abused, in what I must say was a very tiresome way, was not our idea of enjoyment. To people who had chafed under the routine of some less liberal school, or who were of that temperament that cannot be happy at any school,

---

[1] Please note that O.B. and not "the O.B." is the original, and therefore the correct usage.

O.B. was of use and comfort : they will always be grateful to him. And for many others he must have opened doors to knowledge and led them for part of the way along the path.

" Oh, there you are, old man ! How are you ? Come and sit next me in Hall and tell me everything you've been doing ! " This, at the beginning of a term. We are seated and I begin. " Well, I went to France for about three weeks. I was in the south-east most of the time—at Digne and Sisteron. . . ." O.B. sits drumming with his fingers on the table and gazing before him with a lack-lustre eye. When I have spoken for about a minute, he breaks in, " Oh, did you really ? How very interesting ! " (pronounced " veynsing"). " Well, I—I—I—," and for the rest of the meal there is a monologue. Here was the key to the whole business : he never could be really interested in anything but his own concerns. If once he could have pushed past the figure (of O.B.) which bulked so large before him, he might have been a great man. He was undoubtedly a very kind one.

A photographic record of his talk in lighter moments will be found in E. F. Benson's *David of King's*, where he figures as Mr. Gray. The same book has a still better presentment of my next subject, J. E. Nixon. Whether you be a Kingsman or have never heard of King's, you cannot fail to be delighted with Mr. Crowfoot. The memory of Nixon is very kindly. It is

also incredibly comic. Having had, I imagine,
a rough time in College at Eton, he grew up a
very fierce champion of the oppressed. Gradually the fierceness diminished, but the chival-
rous instincts remained. The mind, however,
was like no one else's. It worked like a clock
with the pendulum taken off, or an electric
fan out of order, and the utterance did its best
to keep up with it. The speeches of Mrs.
Nickleby run admirably into Nixonese. As to
the passion for impracticable contrivances which
possessed him, the White Knight in *Through the
Looking Glass* was the standard parallel. Every
small emergency of life was to find him prepared
to meet it, and was to be countered in some
quite unexpected way. His path was beset by
rather more obstacles than most people's, for
he had but one hand (the left) and one eye. One
does not want to make capital out of physical
defects, and I don't think that Nixon ever met
with any rudeness on this account, but you cannot
suppose that we preserved that silence or
unconsciousness about them in his absence
which we did when he was there. They also
form an important element in the picture of him.
Think of him as a small man with a short reddish
beard, habited commonly in a black tail-coat,
and moving rapidly about, on feet which turned
up at the toes rather sharply. The swift
gesture with which he put in place the hinged
glasses attached to his spectacles for reading

purposes was almost the first thing to attract
attention. The posture in which, clasping his
chin with his left hand (ánd fondly assuming that
it would be mistaken for his right), he leaned his
elbow on the cushion of his desk in Chapel,
came next. The sight of him urging a specially
constructed tricycle over King's Bridge would
be another delight of the early days. But indeed
so rich was the harvest yielded to the careful
observer of Nixon's habits, that we often con-
templated the publication of an octavo volume
wholly devoted to the description of these. Here
I have not room for more than a few representative traits.

A very important chapter in the projected
book would have had to deal with the goodness
of Nixon. He went out of the beaten track to
do most of the ordinary things, certainly ; but
to do a kindness he was always going out of his
way, particularly if he took it into his head that
anyone was in danger of being " out of it " : and
if he once made a friend he clave to him, and kept
up with him. He had a railway map of England
cut out of a Bradshaw (and doubtless pasted on
to fragments of Latin proses) upon which he
had marked in red ink all the places where
friends lived, so that if his journeys took him in
their direction he could look in on them between
trains. This was typical both of the goodness
and the oddness: but there were numberless
instances of the goodness which were more

substantial : he was always helping poor men, and, with Augustus Leigh, was a principal mover in the establishment of the Choir School, as well as in the general and enormous improvement of the Chapel services which had been taking place in the years before I came up.   A great deal more could be said about the good deeds of Nixon, but it would have to be collected from the subjects of them.

There is no doubt, however, that the monograph would have been remembered chiefly for its record of the oddnesses.   I really don't know what to choose among my memories for record here.   Nixon was a Dean and a Lecturer on Classics when I came up.   In the former capacity he did not write letters like Augustus Leigh, but employed a printed slip of blue paper: " Mr. *Blank* is requested to call on the Dean in Charge at——on——."   This note was appended: " If the undergraduate sent for is unavoidably prevented from calling at the time named, he is requested to send an explanation and call *as soon as possible at one of the same times on the following day*."   This *may* be all right ; Nixon could have argued for its correctness till he dropped ; but I have always suspected there was something not quite according to Cocker.   My readers must judge.

As Dean, he was concerned, of course, with the Chapel and its services.   Once he moved for the purchase of so many dozen more chairs at a College meeting.   One of the purists whom one always meets in such assemblies said the wording should be " so many dozen *additional* chairs." I do not know how long Nixon argued this grammatical point *viva voce*, for I was not there. But it is certain that after the meeting he wrote and sent round, in what was called hektograph or jellygraph, a paper recapitulating his arguments, and adding that perhaps his opponents would prefer the opening lines of a well-known hymn to run, "A few additional years shall roll, A few additional seasons come."

On the occasion of either Bradshaw's or Provost Okes's funeral in Chapel, Nixon was desirous to know how many people came. Mr. Thomas, the head porter, was to be stationed at the door of entrance for the public. To him Nixon entrusted a bag of beans and another bag of gun-wads. For each person who entered Thomas was to transfer a bean into the gun-wad bag and for each *tenth* person a gun-wad into the bean bag, thus, as Nixon explained, securing a twofold check on the reckoning. But, like so many other bright projects, this was a failure. "Thomas," Nixon complained, "was very stupid about it : he put all the beans and gun-wads together into one bag and couldn't tell me anything. Very disappointing. I strongly suspect he mixed them all up before anyone came in at all." So do I : Thomas, a man of un-exampled dignity, was not likely to demean himself to any such antics.

On the most crowded Sunday afternoon in the
May week I went into Chapel and found the
entrance into the choir congested with a seething
mob. A neighbouring magnate was repeating,
" But I'm Mr. Pemberton of Trumpington,"
and the harassed servant in charge was saying :
" I don't care who you are, Sir, you can't come
in without you've got an order." Suddenly
Nixon entered, hurried up to the crowd and
proclaimed : " Unless all of you leave the Chapel
this moment, there will be no Divine Service
this afternoon." I am afraid the announcement
did not produce the slightest effect. Nixon,
however, was satisfied that he had coped quite
successfully with the situation, and immediately
wrote another hektographed pamphlet " On the
Management of Large Crowds." Shortly after,
the Deanship changed hands, and the entire
regulation and disciplining of visitors was entrusted to our Chapel Clerk, Mr. Walter Littlechild, who told us officials exactly what we were
to do, and never again was there any trouble.

I have said that I owe to Nixon part of my
distaste for business meetings. I have a recollection of one day, before I was a Fellow, when an
all-day sitting of the College Congregation was
going on in the Combination Room. Somebody
passed the windows and saw Welldon leaning
out. He issued this bulletin : " Nixon just up
for the forty-third time." I have not the least
doubt that this was true : he behaved like an

insane Jack-in-the-box, and carried the passion
for debate so far that on one occasion (perhaps
more than one), after speaking for a motion
that stood in his name and reducing the company
to silent apathy, he claimed the right of reply.
It was granted. He replied exhaustively to his
own proposal, and when it was put to the vote
was the only person who voted on the motion:
and voted against it! Can you wonder that he
was elected Gresham Professor of Rhetoric (about
1880, I think) and held the post till his death ?

His oratory was a little difficult to follow. Such
words as " laboratory " he was supposed to be
able to pronounce in one syllable, " fish sauce "
stood for official sources, " hairpin " for high
opinion, " temmince " for ten minutes, and so on.
There was also some mixture of metaphors.
" So far is the College from having all its eggs in
one basket that it may very fairly be said to be
riding on four anchors."

Perhaps he was best at what he called " mooting
a point." Arguments were begun with every
appearance of the strictest method, which, however, under the stress of supervening ideas,
each rejected in favour of the next before any
had found full expression, broke down rather
quickly. " Very well, then, let's go into it
thoroughly. Take the case of a man named
Forbes—or, no—better, perhaps, take the case
of a man named Smith, who says—stay, though,
that wouldn't do. No, of course not ; I have

it. Suppose—I forgot, though ; no, there again
. . . . Well, anyhow . . ." Such was the
exordium, as we thought of it. The combative
spirit in him was strong. You asked whether
he did not approve some proposal. " Certainly
not ! Why, just think " (a sharp clearing of the
throat to gain time : then, still searching for an
objection) " What did you say ? " The notable reply, " Yes, a thousand times yes—or
rather, No, a thousand times no," was one of his
reported oratorical flights : there is, however, no
end to the tale of Nixonisms.

The following incident is typical. Journeying
forth on his tricycle one afternoon for air and
exercise, he came to sad grief at the bottom of the
Madingley hill, was picked up and brought home
and laid up for three weeks. When restored to
health, he went forth again on the mended
tricycle, accompanied by his friend George
Chawner, to survey the scene of the disaster.
" It was just here," he said, " that it happened.
I was merely doing like this . . ." His recollection was doubtless accurate. Over went the
tricycle again, and three weeks more in bed were
the result.

That may be partly mythology : for you cannot
be surprised to hear that a very copious mythology
was built up about Nixon, though it may be
painful to learn—as it should be painful to
confess—that the other protagonist in the myths
was Dr. Westcott. (It was really a tribute to

him that he should have been cast for this rôle : it meant that he was the least possible person.) For this purpose Westcott had to be thought of as Professor Moriarty, " the Napoleon of Crime." It is relevant to mention here that when the play *Sherlock Holmes* was being given at Cambridge I attended a performance with J. W. Clark ; and when the curtain rose on the frail and venerable figure of Professor Moriarty sitting in his lair like the spider in the centre of the web, and organizing atrocities all over the country, " J." whispered to me at once, " Dr. Westcott ! " Well, the Westcott-Nixon myth had many phases. Perhaps Dr. Westcott felt it his duty to make a first-hand study of the terrible evils of gambling at Monte Carlo. It would be Nixon who, most handsomely, defrayed the entire expenses of the trip, and, most unfortunately, was the victim of an almost unprecedented run of ill-luck at the tables. It would be Nixon, again, who caused a momentary disturbance at the Jubilee of 1887 by falling from the triforium of the Abbey, where he had been accommodated with a precarious seat by Dr. Westcott, then Canon of Westminster : or who, in later years when staying at Auckland, was recorded to have plumbed the depths of almost every coal-mine in the district in a series of the quickest descents on record. No one could have expressed keener regret at these untoward accidents than Dr. Westcott : but a sinister fate seemed to dog the footsteps of the pair : they hardly ever met without Nixon's experiencing either in purse or in person some (too often literally) crippling misadventure.

It was sometimes difficult to reconcile with the known kindliness of Dr. Westcott's nature happenings such as his upsetting of a hive of bees in Nixon's rooms and then quickly leaving the staircase.   But in all such cases (and there were not a few of them) one had recourse to the comforting reflection that Dr. Westcott was a firm believer in the disciplinary value of Suffering.

The attitude of Nixon, as imagined by the mythologists, was that of one a good deal flattered by the attentions of Dr. Westcott, putting a good face on all these mishaps and regarding or affecting to regard them as purely accidental. " Of course it was rather painful at the time; still, it was all very pleasant, and one learnt a good deal."

Let me excuse the introduction of this fantasy by the plea that it may be of considerable interest to students of folk-lore.   That serves to carry off most things nowadays.

The equipment and the course of a glee meeting at Nixon's have been nobly recorded in *David of King's*. We derived the keenest pleasure from the performance of the item " Of all the Brave Birds that ever I see."   In this there is a line (Cinnamon and ginger, nutmeg and cloves) wherein the first syllable of the word ginger is prolonged for several bars on a single high note. It was regularly arranged that this part should be taken by Nixon. " Oh, but I can't do that alone." So some others volunteered. " Now, mind, you must support me " (he was a little suspicious about this particular piece). But somehow all the voices suddenly failed when Cinnamon was reached, and Nixon was invariably left making a noise like a distant siren and diligently beating time with a paperknife. " Too bad, really. We must have that again. Let me see, what was the note ? Better take it in A flat this time." A rapid dash to the piano followed and several adjacent notes were struck, after which the ritual was gone through again.

As years went on, the fierceness which had characterized Nixon melted away : he no longer " protested most strongly " at College meetings, or rebuked the Bursar for breaking into a " rude guffaw." More and more he responded to the real affection that was felt for him, and in his last years was the centre of an always amused but sincerely devoted circle of the young. The perplexities and anxieties of the War and the loss of many of those young friends finally broke his gallant spirit.

I may deal more shortly with others of the seniors who did not often cross our path. Churton was one of these, the Rev W. R. Churton, B.D., a man of great saintliness of life and an unwearied worker for the Church abroad. His rooms were the centre of many religious meetings : in fact, one large sitting-room was permanently set out with chairs for this purpose. The great Simeon, who once occupied the adjacent rooms (Fred Whitting's in my time), would not at all have approved the ecclesiastical complexion of Churton's meetings : they were at the opposite pole of thought to his.

Churton was most regularly to be seen in early hours hurrying across the grass of the front court to take a service in the town. It was noted that he never could remember that (in the year 1879) a fountain had been placed in the centre of this plot. He always started to go straight across to the gate, and then, suddenly aware of the fountain, swerved to the right. " Churton's path " was very clearly marked in the grass. His clothes (we believed) were made by a tailor of drunken habits whom he was trying to reclaim : whether this was so or not, the artist was always grudging in the matter of cloth for the trousers. Churton was not often seen in Hall : he preferred a " hegg in his rooms," as his bedmaker lamented ; and when there he was habitually rather silent : how absurd it is that the only remark of his at the High Table that I can quote was when, talking about edible snails, I said I didn't suppose you could get them in England, and Churton at once told me the name of a shop in London where they were to be had !

An occasional but quite frequent visitor was

William Austen Leigh, youngest of the brothers, a clerk in the House of Lords and long one of the three Bursars.   He kept rooms in College which were in frequent demand for guests, and always attended important College meetings.   He played beautifully on the excellent piano in those rooms and gave us many a pleasant evening there : fostering in me an innate love of Handel, whose works he knew well.   Like his brothers he was a generous benefactor to the College : the first Choral Scholars we had were provided for by funds given by the Austen Leighs, and Willy regularly made over the dividends of his Fellowship (as did Edward also) for College purposes. With him one classes Felix Cobbold—once Bursar—the director of bank, brewery and wine businesses at Ipswich—the soul of liberality.   It was customary for Cobbold, Willy and Edward Leigh, Richard and Walter Durnford and Arthur Morton (the well-known private-school master) to assemble at King's about Christmas time.   The party, augmented by others, such as Frank Tarver and Ainger, used to move on to the Lodge at Felixstowe and keep New Year there in the height of comfort.   When I attained years of discretion, Felix was good enough to include me and others of younger generations in these delightful parties.   Those who were not strong enough, or not weak enough, to play golf (which most of them did all day) had a very happy time : Fred Whitting and I would occupy a whole

morning over a game of fifty up at billiards :
misses and pocketing one's own ball made up
the bulk of the score.   But I wander.

A strange figure in the person of H. N.
Mozley came into residence, from chambers in
London, not late in the 'eighties.   Long years of
solitary life had made him very eccentric, but
he was full of good-will, particularly to the
undergraduates, and they responded nobly.
Breakfast parties were his speciality : in the
invitations to them the names of everyone you
were to meet were carefully given, and their
Colleges. l have a recollection of a party at
which Percival Hart Dyke, who was blind, was
present. Mozley, always shy, was greatly embarrassed (Hart Dyke not in the least) and
danced about, saying to others of the party :
" Would he like some tea, do you think ?   Does
he eat bread and butter ? "—for of course if a
man was blind he must be deaf and dumb as
well. He had one of those curious memories
which retain all facts equally clearly. He could
remember what the dinner in Hall had been on
a given day a year before, and if you made a
verbal appointment with him for a particular
hour months ahead he would be there on the
tick, not aided by any such thing as an engage-
ment book. But the most repaying of his
oddities to the heartless youth was this.   They
sat at their window looking out into the court and
saw Mozley coming out of his staircase, intent

on a brisk walk. They then gave a low but penetrating whistle. Mozley started, looked round and stopped dead, and if the whistle was repeated ran back into his staircase like a rabbit. In a minute or two he would peep out again, looking cautiously about. Again they whistled, of course keeping themselves concealed : again he ran back. The unkind creatures would—if no better amusement offered—keep the poor gentleman running to and fro for an entire afternoon by this simple expedient. It was believed, and I hope it is true, that he never detected the source of the whistling. In other ways the youths were very considerate, and by their help he passed several quite happy years at King's.

Are dons as odd nowadays as they were then ? It can hardly be. Most of them are married and live normal family lives : which is no doubt an excellent thing, but, if I may air a grievance, makes Collegiate life a very different and a rather difficult affair. Where Fellowships are many, there is always a hope that some will elect to spend their days in College : where they are few, it may be—it is—the case that no Fellow makes his home there for more than the agreed number of nights in the term. The centre of gravity of his affections and interests runs a great risk of being shifted from the College to the villa. But do not let the married don imagine that he cannot be a figure of fun to the undergraduate: though it is doubtless the bachelor Fellow, living all his days in College, who has the best chance of developing strange tricks and becoming a subject of careful observation in consequence. I think the most pathetic utterance of Oscar Browning that ever I heard was to this effect: " I far prefer life among undergraduates to life among schoolboys : schoolboys always laugh at one, undergraduates don't." Yet he was a clever man.

I have now said as much as I think proper—perhaps more than other people will think proper—about the elder population of King's as I found it in 1882. It may be time to revert to my own experiences and contemporaries.

XIII

I HAVE said that the body of undergraduates which I joined consisted of 67 persons—Eton Scholars, Open Scholars, Exhibitioners, Choral Scholars, Pensioners : these were the categories. By Pensioners were meant ordinary undergraduates. Everyone at King's except the Choral Scholars was (and is) obliged to be a candidate for Honours, *i.e.* to go in for a Tripos and not take an ordinary or Pass or Poll degree.

How was one received into this body ? The Eton Scholar found old friends at once, of course, and these asked him in to breakfast or lunch or coffee after Hall, to meet new friends. At Pembroke and some other Colleges there was a rigid system by which all senior undergraduates left cards on the freshman, and the freshman was obliged to return these calls and go on till he found the caller at home. We had no such rule, and were not too numerous to be all invited at various times to other people's rooms : it being the tradition that everyone should at least have a chance of knowing everyone else.

Need I say that there were rifts ? Some Etonians were suspicious of non-Etonians, feeling, perhaps, that their old sacred preserve was being laid waste by revolutionaries. Some non-Etonians were suspicious of Etonians, anticipating that we should " suspend them from an adunc nose " (as Bradshaw would say, pressing the tip of that feature with his finger the while). There was undeniably an Eton clique, though it included many who were not from Eton. I could tell unedifying and uninteresting stories of collisions such as youth rather welcomes and enjoys. Our elders saw, and regretted, and did all they could to heal, breaches : but of course some irreconcilables on both sides stood out. Later years showed all the parties concerned that there had been a good deal of foolishness in their early views of each other ; but probably everyone would allow that at some stage of the development of the College a cleavage must have come. Doubtless New College has seen Wykehamists and non-Wykehamists playing very similar parts. Enough of that.

I found myself for the first year lodged in rooms in King's Lane, in a house adapted to College purposes not long before, and provided with its own porter, who had to let you across the lane to College at all hours. Now there is a sub-way. The rooms are not lordly, but were pleasant enough to one coming from school. The bed-maker's help, Hannah Harvey, deserves commemoration for great gallantry of spirit. She retired after long service, crippled with rheuma-tism. She could hardly move : but when my

friend E. G. Swain as curate of St. Mary's
visited her, and one day condoled with her, she
said, "After all, it's all a bit o' fun, ain't it, Sir?"
This I call heroism.

Prothero and Welldon were the Tutors : the
latter soon left King's for Dulwich, but the
former was in office till 1893, and no kinder, no
more diligent ruler could we have had. His
admirable *Memoir* of Bradshaw gives a key to his
own character as well as that of his subject.
Sympathetic with Old King's and ardently
interested in New King's, he used his influence
to combine jarring elements, and as a teacher
besides was largely responsible for securing the
prominence of the College in historical studies.

Welldon, living in Fellows' Buildings—Gibbs's
Building—kept a sharp look-out from his windows, and it was a hazardous business to cross the
court in the morning hours, for Welldon might
intercept you and express an anxious hope that
you had not received any bad news to call you
away from your work at that time of day. This
was very wholesome. Also I cannot praise him
too highly for the care he lavished on our written
work. He was an excellent Tutor.

A page about Work must follow here, I see.
There are some who derive benefit from formal
lectures on a classical text : I was one who did
not, or thought I did not, which comes to the
same. Paper work, translation and composition,
was a very different thing, indispensable, and

very well cared for.   But for making acquaintance
with the ancient literature I felt I was best left
to myself.   The ambition was to read everything,
not dwelling on minutiæ, and not being very
particular as to the date of an author.

I don't think it is at all a bad ambition, either,
if you have the instinct for it.   However, I
need hardly say it was not realized.   It soon
became obvious that technical philosophy was
not to be mastered in that way.   Large regions
of Aristotle and Plato had to be left unexplored,
and there were other departments of literature,
not so intrinsically difficult, which defied the
amateur just as effectively by their dulness.
Xenophon's *Hellenica* I take to be the stodgiest
of all Greek history books, and how the orations
of Isæus (which I *did* read under compulsion),
entirely concerned as they are with disputed
wills and heiresses, ever got or kept their reputation I cannot conceive.   But these snags were
few in comparison with the dozens of writers
who could be devoured, some with ease and
comfort, some at a slower pace.   The insight into
the mind and atmosphere of Greece and Rome
which one gained may not have been—was not—
the clearest or most accurate, but it was very
extensive and very precious, and the process of
acquiring it was blissful.   The paper-work kept
up the standard of accuracy, and taught me to be
on my guard against expressions proper to the
third and fourth centuries.   The excursions

into those and into much later centuries I have never regretted, and I commend them to the youth of the present day : to whom I also say, " You ought to aim at being able to take the general sense of a page of Greek or Latin as easily as that of a page of French."

I do not think that all this reading was very much influenced by the prospect of examinations. No doubt I did go in for prizes and scholarships, and was much pleased when I was successful, but about the Tripos I did not think much, and was, indeed, quite uncertain what it meant and when it was coming on. What appeared to be important was the finding out about things that interested me ; and since these things included my proper and prescribed work, all was well.

At this time the Classical Tripos had recently been divided into two parts. In the first you were examined in pure classics ; this you might take in your second year, as I did : in the second, besides an obligatory section of translation and composition, you took up a special section devoted to Philosophy or History or Archæology or Philology. Mine was Archæology. From Dr. Waldstein (Sir Charles Walston), lecturing on Greek Sculpture, I learnt, it is safe to say, more than I ever did from any other lecturer on any subject. He made you see, and he inspired enthusiasm. At this time, too, at the expense of a short period of drudgery with a dictionary, I became able to use German books. For this purpose it is quite unnecessary to go and live in Dresden : that is all very well if you want to talk the language, but for my part the more I read of it the less I wanted to speak it, for it has suffered dreadful things in the last two centuries at the hands of savants and (as used by them) has become a very ugly machine, though quite indispensable to anyone who aspires to be a scientific student of I care not what department of learning.

So that was the course of academic studies. There were plenty of other fields of learning into which I trespassed, but they can wait. Let me return to the story of life apart from books.

The day began at 8 a.m. with a struggle. Either Chapel must be attended, or your name must be signed in a book at the Porter's Lodge before the clock had finished striking eight. When it was the Scholar's week to read a lesson in Chapel (and grace in Hall) the claims of Chapel were superior. And in some other weeks one did contrive to be regularly there. But " signing-in " was a tempting alternative, for it required but a great-coat and trousers, beneath which it were ill to inquire too closely what lay hid, and a run across the court. As the process has long been obsolete, nobody but myself can be hurt by the confession that I never once signed-in without going back to bed afterwards. The failure of the rule to promote permanent early-rising has led to the substitution of frequent nine o'clock lectures, which I am glad to say were not prevalent in my day. Breakfast, solitary in one's rooms, or with a party. Beer was a usual finale of the more formal parties at this date—beer in a silver tankard from College—but its popularity was on the wane. At Pembroke, I will note, they offered you copus, a sort of beer-cup, to which Gray alludes in his letters : more interesting than palatable. The kitchens were farmed out in most Colleges : the bills for extra provender being in the nature of ordinary tradesmen's accounts. With us the family of Lawrance had been long in possession. Now every College, so far as I know, runs its own kitchen with a salaried staff. Lectures might endure from ten to one ; lunch, not an elaborate affair if you were alone, followed. And then we come to the question of games. I don't believe I ever once played football at Cambridge. For about three weeks in my first term I went down to the river on most days to be tubbed. Then there came an afternoon when it sleeted and was piercingly cold, and the feelings of repulsion for the Cam and its surroundings which had long been festering within me broke out. I said " Never again," and stuck to that. To be short, I played no games, nor wanted to. The accomplishment of riding a high bicycle—the only form of the instrument then possible—I tried to master, but with no success. So the afternoons, when other people went to the river or the fields, had no prescribed duties for me : probably the most energetic thing I did was to take quite long walks and make acquaintance with most of the villages about Cambridge. But it would be no sin in my eyes to spend the time in a library. Dusk fell (I am thinking now of October and November) and one might seek the rooms of a friend in King's or Trinity for tea, or, if engaged to read lessons, would repair to King's Chapel at five. Often enough I would go there uncompelled. But the time for discoursing about Chapel is not yet.

I believe that in those days Hall was at six : I cannot remember how soon it slipped on to seven and to half-past seven. In any case it was the next outstanding feature. No set places were assigned, of course. The several years were apt to congregate and informally appropriate certain tables, but the lines were not strictly drawn between year and year. Twenty minutes sufficed for dinner ; part of it will have been occupied in sending notes about to invite people to coffee afterwards. It was a rule almost invariable that you did not go straight back to work, even the most relentless of you, but to some appointed rooms where you met your friends or did the civil thing to new comers over coffee and a liqueur. Also, that after discussing these you worked for maybe two hours and then sought company again. If it was an out-college friend you wanted, you must of course rush out at five minutes to ten, or you would not

be able to get into the college or the lodgings :
once there, you would very likely stay till close
on midnight. If it was in College that you were
wasting a friend's time, there was nothing to
prevent you doing so till the dawn of another
day. At the end of the *séance*, on a fine night,
you would perambulate the court. It is at
twenty minutes to two a.m. that you may hear
in late October the wild geese coming over
King's. The sound is at first that of small
birds twittering over Clare: then it passes high
in air from north-west to south-east.

Such was the course of a normal week-day in
1882 : subject, to be sure, to innumerable varia-
tions, such as meetings of societies, lunches or
dinners with Fellows or undergraduates, concerts,
incursions of the outer world : never (thank
Heaven) to the informal dances, or the drawing-
room calls, which I am told play a large part
in undergraduate life now. But my ideals of
University life have always been sadly monastic.

Sunday was different. More often than not
it began with a breakfast party in the regions of
nine o'clock. Morning Chapel was at ten, and
had to be kept. There were dreadful, wicked
creatures who postponed their breakfast until
after Chapel. During my first year or so
lunch was an informal club affair : the same eight
or nine people met every week, and one of them
provided lunch for the rest. This was prejudicial to a regular attendance at the University

sermon at two, yet one often did go when the preacher was famous. Our Chapel followed, at 3.30, and the rest of the day was all our own. Before very long the Sunday supper ousted the Sunday lunch, for Hall was not popular on this day. Whatever form dinner took, it was followed by some sort of gathering, large or small. It was on Sunday evenings that assemblages—adequately described by E. F. Benson—took place in Oscar Browning's rooms : on Sundays, I think, that Harry Cust would summon all his wide acquaintance to what he called a Hell in his rooms at Trinity : the name indicates the miscellaneous nature of the company. More agreeable than either was a collection of half a dozen familiars, entailing no journey through dark streets and no encounters with imperfectly known persons ; this in course of time became more stereotyped.

XIV

ACQUAINTANCES multiplied rapidly, partly through the ordinary post-prandial meetings in other people's rooms, partly by means of the Pitt, to which I was elected in due course, but as much as anything by means of the drama. In my first term the first Greek play of a long series was produced, the *Ajax*, with J. K. Stephen in the title-rôle. His acting was long remembered : it seemed afterwards a sad presage that he, whose great brain was in the end stricken, should have had to present that particular part. Harry Cust as Teucer and A. R. Macklin as Tecmessa were only less memorable because Ajax is so dominant. Well, many friends took part in the *Ajax*, and it was a great event, but I was no more than a spectator. Very soon in 1883 the Committee who managed these things decided on a comedy, the *Birds* of Aristophanes, and I was cast for the longest part, that of Peithetairos. In October we began on the business seriously, with Heaven knows how many rehearsals of single scenes and whole acts per week. As I was on in almost every scene, much of this went on in my rooms (which were now a large set in Fellows' Buildings). I don't suppose I ever spent a more

consistently amusing term : there was shaking
of heads over the inroads into my working time,
but in the end nobody seemed one penny the
worse.

I was indubitably the better. Not only did
I swim into the ken of such great ones as J. W.
Clark, Henry Jackson, Stanford, Hubert Parry,
Waldstein, Verrall, but enlarged very quickly and
in the easiest way my circle of out-college
friends. About the performances themselves,
which took up a week in the end of November,
there is a halo in memory. In part the halo is
literal, for it was the time of the Krakatoa
sunsets : to anyone who remembers them the
name is enough : anyone who does not I can't
help. There has been nothing since like the
sight we used to see as we came out of evening
Chapel and looked across the lawn to the belt
of leafless trees and the blazing sky.

But besides this there was Hubert Parry's
delicious music, including the Wedding March
celebrating the union of Peithetairos with Basileia
(Ernest Gardner), which must be one of the
best things of its kind in existence, and the
Nightingale's Song, quite wonderfully sung by
G. J. Maquay. There were the delights of
watching Harry Newton as Euelpides, Sir R.
Threlfall in the part of Herakles, Tatham as the
Triballian god, Dighton Pollock as Iris : of
hearing Platts's fine rendering of the Parabasis :
there were the anxieties which attended the

appearance of Harry Cust (Prometheus), who had never committed any portion of his lines to memory, and had to get them from me as occasion offered, filling in the gaps with improvisation in an unknown tongue—and clad moreover in but one garment snatched up at the last moment : the satisfaction I derived from scourging the bare calves of the Sycophant (Sir Laurence Guillemard) and listening to his fervid comments in the vernacular—a privilege denied to the audience. In short, the whole week was amazingly pleasant, and when it was over life seemed a very hollow thing.

It was after this that I joined the A.D.C. and its Committee, which lunched on Sundays at the rooms of the members in rotation, J. W. Clark being always present. At this time the A.D.C. confined itself to what may be called without offence the lower walks of the drama. There was no Ibsen, no Pirandello (which may not be surprising) : Shakespeare was not attempted till 1886. The principal effort in my day was *The Overland Route* (not, I think, really a very good play), in which I sustained the part of Sir Solomon Fraser, an elderly Anglo-Indian, who, wrecked on a desert island, loses his denture and is reduced to sad straits. The A.D.C. was a great source of amusement and another enlarger of acquaintance. It brought me into contact with an acting society at St. John's called the Thespids or Thespians (long since dead, I

suppose), which had a periodical dinner followed
by a performance in College rooms. The *Foot-
lights*, still vigorous, was founded about this
time : it was fashionable in A.D.C. circles to
regard it as an Upstart.

I will now for the time being leave the subject
of the drama, only adding that the next Greek
plays, *Eumenides* of 1885 and *Oedipus Tyrannus*
of 1887, were the last in which I took any part.
But, however ill it becomes me, I shall not shrink
from writing of my own dramatic productions
of a somewhat later time, for I am sure nobody
else will be found to celebrate them as they
deserve.

The year 1885 had one great revelation for me.
In March my eldest brother and Walter Durnford combined to frank me on an expedition
to Greece, of which the other members were
Stuart and St. Clair Donaldson and Cecil
Baring. Impossible to exaggerate the enjoyment of this : impossible to impart it. What is
the name of a place somewhere near Andritzena
where the Alpheus river bursts out from under
a rock, and a large wild fig-tree grows over it?
Labda, I am told. That is the spot I should feel
inclined to haunt, and that is the kind of picture
which in the end one treasures most. You are
prepared in some degree for the buildings and
the sculptures, but not for the context of them
and the landscape.

Between 1880 and the War no year passed

without my being abroad somewhere. As I have said, my tutor introduced me to French cathedrals in 1880 : I determined as soon as opportunity offered to improve the acquaintance. At the end of June 1884 Hugh Childers and I hired a strange machine called a Cheylesmore double tricycle, and embarked with it at the Port of London for Boulogne. I have never seen the like of the creature since : we sat side by side : the steering gear was in front, controlled by a ratchet contrivance worked by a handle resembling that of a child's spade. The tyres were solid. With infinite labour we urged this vehicle through Abbeville, Amiens, Noyon, Laon, Rheims, Chalons, Troyes, Sens, Auxerre, to Avallon in Yonne. The days were of the hottest, and the Cheylesmore, having received an awkward bump on board the boat, was always breaking its spokes, which no village blacksmith whom we consulted (and they were many in their numbers) could succeed in stabilizing for more than ten minutes. All horses shied at our approach : when we encountered a stretch of paved road (common in Aisne and Marne) we at once struck up the 109th psalm ("Set thou an ungodly man to be ruler over him"), so that, what with the invocations of the market-women and our own *devotiones* of the road-makers, our path was blasted with maledictions. It was, for all that, singularly delightful. The bathes in wayside streams : the drinks, the foods : the wide prospects from

the tops of hills at night (for we often ploughed on
till very late), the smell of vineyards in flower in
early morning : the sighting of the next cathedral
tower above the poplars, and the subsequent
deciphering and noting of all its sculpture and
glass—which sounds like bathos, but is nothing
of the kind.   I have not often been more acutely
alive in mind and body.   One detail of travel
comes back, and that is the great difficulty
there was in finding the way on anything but a
Route Nationale.   There were very few maps:
the French ordnance was on such a large scale
that a sheet lasted you only a few miles, and the
chances were that the next sheet was not to be
had.   So there was often great uncertainty about
route and, particularly, distances, as to which the
population, especially the women, were but ill
informed.   Nobody can complain of that now who
lives under the dispensation of M. Taride and
M. Michelin.

The trip of 1884 settled the question as to what
was to be the holiday country.   After a little
toying with train and tricycle, the mode of travel
was also settled in 1895 by the advent of the
" safety " bicycle and the pneumatic tyre.   Hence-
forth every year contributed its fortnight at
Easter, and in most cases its three weeks or month
in summer as well.   The choice of a route was
regulated by the presence of cathedrals or former
cathedrals.   In 1790 you may reckon that there
were upwards of 140 bishoprics in the 85 depart-

ments of pre-War France (excluding Alsace-Lorraine, but including Savoy and 'Alpes Maritimes). A few have accrued since : before the War I put the total at 143, of which I visited all but two (Nice and Toulon, if anyone cares to know). Some of these take a good deal of finding, and when found do not detain the traveller for many minutes. Of such is Vabres, which with Glandéves I count among the rarest specimens. Glandéves is not discoverable upon all maps : it is reduced to the apse of the church, used as a barn, and standing by the road from Entrevaux to Puget-Theniers. Of such again is Bethléem. The choir of the cathedral served in 1910 as the *salle à manger* of a hotel in Clamecy.

Who shall duly celebrate the excellences of the push-bike tour in France, particularly in the years before the War ? Over thirty times I did it, so I do not speak without knowledge : but, after all, who wants to know—what the companions of the voyage never tire of conning over—the little sorrows and the greater joys (not least of food and drink) which enlivened the business for us ? I have seen men of *great eminence* in the community placed in very humiliating situations : it would not need much provocation to make me reveal the names of a party of such men, who played at least one rubber of Bridge with a pack from which all the Knaves had been removed, and *never discovered it*. The explanations which came later varied between the statements that they did not believe it and that they had known it all the time.

In leaving the subject of France I should like to record, in a spirit of cynical superiority, that I always declined to *do* the châteaux on the Loire, but that I have more or less explored every department except one—the Ardennes.

XV

As far as these small-beer chronicles have any plan, it is chronological, but I allow a topic which comes up in its proper place to take me with it as far as it will. The last one started in 1884. I have said that by that time (in fact, in October 1883) I had moved into larger rooms. They were on the ground floor of Gibbs's Building (staircase next to Chapel, left-hand side). I succeeded Arthur Benson, one of whose recent predecessors had been J. K. Stephen. Here I came under the influence of Mrs. Ann Smith, one of the greatest and best of bedmakers: rather tall, rather austere in aspect, always to be seen in a bonnet, and in a crinoline. Her " help," described as her daughter, though the family tree was never fully known to me, was equally virtuous and more rugged in face. An excellent parishioner, among other things, was Mrs. Smith. She glowed with satisfaction on being introduced to her Vicar's new wife, who seemed, she said, to be so very 'ighly domesticated. I had, too, occasional reports of his sermons: " He coated the Miraculous Draught of Fishes, Sir, and beautiful indeed did he enlarge upon it." Without being importunate, she did a lot of modest collecting for charities from her gentlemen, Dr. Barnardo being the favourite. Not unsympathetic, either, was she with human weaknesses : when I have rushed to early Chapel, found the door fastened, and come back dismally, " Ah, Sir, how often I've seen Mr. Nixon flit up to the door like that and come away again." *Flit* was the *mot juste*. But her speech was often noteworthy. " Well, Sir, that's my masterpiece," was one of her good phrases—when she found she couldn't pull up the blind or achieve some like feat. " Them little hurchin lads " was another, applied to the errand boys whom she suspected of purloining one's cigarettes. Politics I don't think she studied much, but after a General Election she has said to me,"Well, Sir, for as simple as I am, I've always heard there was never better times than when the Conservatives was in power." At this time I used to keep a kitten, which travelled about the court on the top of my cap, making an occasional dab at my eye, and it was of this one, I think, that Mrs. Smith would say that it looked at her as deep as a well. The next cat I had much longer, on the top floor of the staircase. She slept on my pillow and caused trouble by walking round and round in my cold bath as soon as the water was poured out, but long before I had any views about getting up. This was not like the poor cat in the adage or like any other cat I have known. Her end was sad. She fell from my

window-box when I was away, and broke bones :
kind people carried her up to the room opposite
mine, but she would crawl across the passage
to die at home.

Of the traditions of the College I only gleaned
one bit from Mrs. Smith. She said there was
an old Mr. Barrett who lived in rooms she
pointed out (they are now a lecture room on
Staircase A) and kept his coffin there : and one
day he was found dead in it. It was implied
that there was something not natural in this.
I think she must have got the name wrong, for
I believe Mr. Richard Barrett, author of a
Synopsis Criticorum (and other works), died at
one of the College livings : but I would not
reject the whole statement. The ancient men
were quite odd enough. Was there not Mr.
Hunt, the contemporary, but not the friend, of
Simeon ? The grimmest of the stories about
him are too grim to be set down—but this
may be recorded. There was adjoining the old
demolished Hall of King's a small room called
the Bursars' Parlour, where two or three seniors
dined together, including Hunt and Simeon.
No one of them, it is said, was on speaking
terms with any other, but one supposes that
occasionally a remark must have been made,
for once Hunt was heard to say, ". . . Mr.
Simeon, Sir, why do you call me an atheist ?
I never called you a humbug." His last will
was quoted as containing an injunction to bury

him in St. Giles's churchyard, " not in the Chapel, where Mr. Simeon lies."

Was there not also Mr. Pote, who occupied a ground floor set at the south end of Gibbs's Building ?   The large outer room, as Sir George Humphry has told me, was totally unfurnished, and given up to dogs and other creatures, with hideous results.   And Mr. Bendyshe, whom I might have seen, for he survived into the 'eighties. He was the most virulent person I remember to have heard of.   My father has told me that his language when he coxed the King's boat (he was a little man) was an ineffaceable memory.   I think of him as something like Quilp.   He could not well enter the College in his latter years, for the Visitor had directed the Provost to reprimand him on the next occasion of his presenting himself at a College meeting.   The crime was a profane letter he had sent to the Dean.   The reprimand was written on a sheet of paper, which folded sheet Provost Okes used always to take with him to a meeting and lay at his right hand, ready for use if Bendyshe appeared.   At one time he edited a paper called the *Reflector*, which was so outrageous in its sentiments that the compositors refused to set up the copy. It finally died owing to an odd blunder of Bendyshe's.   Robert Gordon Latham (of King's), a pioneer in the study of the science of language, produced an edition of Johnson's Dictionary, including the author's preface.   This preface

Bendyshe happened to attribute to Latham, whom he hated, and reviewed it in his most slashing manner. That was the end of the *Reflector*. More about Bendyshe you may find if you wish in the *Memoir* of Bradshaw and that of Augustus Leigh.

But, as I was going to say, perhaps the person whom Mrs. Smith called Mr. Barrett *was* found in his coffin one morning : and perhaps *other hands* laid him there. Ghosts and ghostly phenomena are rare in Colleges, and highly suspect when they do occur. Yet, on the staircase next to mine was a ghostly cry in the bedroom. I never heard it—never, indeed, heard *of* it until a visitor of mine staying in those rooms one Christmas described it at breakfast. Then certain seniors, Fred Whitting and Felix Cobbold, showed no surprise : *they* knew about it, and knew whose voice it was believed to be— that of a man who died in 1878. They had kept it to themselves, and I shall not put it into print.

XVI

It is clearly out of the question to make up lists of all the friends who at this time were part of one's life. As a rule I shall not write much about anyone who is still alive. If this book has an index, and if some of my best friends begin by looking at it (as I so often do myself) to see if their names occur in it, and are disappointed at not finding them, I can do nothing but sympathize. It will not be because they are forgotten, nor will it be because they are not remarkable enough to be put in, that they are left out. The reason will be that a certain shyness, which I cannot explain or defend, comes over me when I begin praising the living. So, if a surviving friend is an actor in an episode which I find it convenient to put in, he will appear; if not, not. Friends will please accept this, the only, intimation.

After which I proceed to chronicle the arrival of two such persons in 1883—Hugessen and Leo Maxse. After a year, I suppose, in King's Lane, Hugessen took the rooms opposite mine at the top of the staircase I have described. I had once again succeeded Arthur Benson in my set, which he had decorated after his own fashion with mottoes and other designs of uncertain import. On a cupboard door, for instance, was an outline in blue of a nude man on a rock, roused by a beam of light striking his brow. On this was written " φῶς ἐθεασάμην καὶ ἔμφοβος ἦν."

Hugessen, I said, was my next-door neighbour. We spent most ordinary evenings doing our work together, and parted in the small hours with the invariable password, " Breakfast at a quarter to nine sharp ? " " Right," for we breakfasted alternately in each other's rooms. Whatever illusions Mrs. Smith and we ourselves may have cherished at one time about these assignations must soon have faded. The written order, indeed, was left out on the table, and the breakfast appeared. It might be an hour later, or it might be less, that the host of the morning would hear the complaining voice of the guest from the outer room, and the reassuring word of Mrs. Smith, " I've just rapped him, Sir." Could there be a blessing on days so begun ? It seems unlikely, but somehow we prospered. There were days in November and January when Nature seemed to have given up the weather business entirely to an amateur. We would then (following a custom begun in College at Eton) " make night " after breakfast by the simple process of drawing the curtains, lighting all available lights and sporting the door. If, in the course of the afternoon, something like normal daylight chose to come on, we might acquiesce and go out. There are still days on which I am only restrained from this practice by the certainty that some visitor of the last importance would force his way in.

Leo Maxse I compare with all affection to a continuously active squib introduced into our calm academic life, but I don't know that I can back up the metaphor by many examples. There was an open debate at the Union on the question whether the Rugby team should or should not be allowed a full Blue. They had, I suppose, a half-blue, like the Lacrosse or Chess or—I know not what. The officials of the Boat Club (C.U.B.C.) were the fountain of honour : at some date known to history but not to me they had granted the Blue to the University Eleven, but they were opposed to making it commoner. Maxse was persuaded without much difficulty to take on the cause of the Rugby team. The President of the C.U.B.C. was no orator : perhaps he too had secured a ready advocate, but if so, it availed not against Maxse's deplorably unscrupulous line, which was to feign ignorance of the meaning of the great initials, and assume that they stood for Cambridge University Bicycle Club. What right, he asked, what conceivable right, had the President of the Cambridge University Bicycle Club to dictate, etc., etc. The angry cries of " Boat Club," " Boat Club," fell on unheeding ears : he ploughed slowly on, reiterating the words " Cambridge University Bicycle Club " with scathing contempt, till the tables were dissolved in laughter : the Blue was granted, of course, in the end.

There was a ridiculous paper—edited by a ridiculous man—called the *Whirlwind*, which once offered a prize for the ugliest man—coupons with votes to be sent in by readers. Maxse exerted his whole influence to bringing in Oscar Browning at the head of the poll, and with complete success. I am a little afraid that he hoped O.B. would be annoyed, but if he was, he knew better than to show it : and, indeed, it was too extravagant to annoy. The silver snuff-box which he won was long exhibited, with explanations, to all visitors.

Maxse and I received so much hospitality from various out-college people, and dining clubs, that we agreed we must combine to return it. So we established a dining club of our own on the approved footing. There was the Trinity Hall *Crescent*, so we called ours the *King's Cross*. It had its ribbon worn across the shirt front with the device in purple : its motto σύνδειπνοῦντες, its bound book of Rules, which prescribed that the membership should be restricted to us two, though Dighton Pollock was eventually admitted by some hanky-panky as Succentor to the Club : that each member might invite six guests : and that certain persons were *ex-officio* excluded from being invited : of whom I remember only the Public Orator, the George Long Prizeman, and Mr. Oscar Browning. It is to be feared that these ceremonies were not devised in that spirit of solemnity which rather amused us in the case of some of the older clubs.

At the time when the Lefroy murder was in everyone's mouth (Lefroy had killed an old gentleman in the Brighton train) Maxse took occasion to see a friend off at Cambridge station, and observed that the only other person in the carriage was an elderly man. So he waited till the train began to move, and then said loudly and cheerfully to his poor friend, " Well, good-bye, Lefroy : I hope they'll let your brother off." First stop, Bishop's Stortford. Not very considerate, I think ?

A particularly amiable and trustful undergraduate was invited, I remember, to Maxse's rooms to meet an emissary from Salt Lake City who would expound the principles of Mormonism. He eagerly accepted, and a few friends rallied round as well. Maxse then introduced the missionary, a gentleman in a beard and spectacles, carrying a large framed and glazed photograph of Jerusalem. But I am sorry to say the part was but ill enacted. Dighton Pollock, for it was he who was reluctantly cast for it, was too kind-hearted and too entirely ignorant of the Message of Mormonism to make any way with the proselytizing ; besides, he will forgive me for saying that he could never hope to earn a living wage by dissimulation.

William Boyle was a great resource : I have said a little of his musical proclivities. They were, of course, greatly extended at King's. His greatest idol was perhaps Handel, but he was also a fervent student of Purcell, of what are now called folk-songs, and of Arne and his like. Thanks to him I was made acquainted with the *Beggar's Opera, Polly,* and the *Jovial Crew*[1] at an early stage, as well as with Chappell's two volumes of Old English Melodies and a large range of the less known Handel. With Dr. Mann he compiled in 1884 the King's College Chant-book that is still in use. Probably there is no more interesting collection of Anglican chants : it was compiled with infinite pains from a very large number of sources. Difficulties of copyright and consequent expense prevented the book from being printed, so it still lives only in lithograph, made from Dr. Mann's beautiful neat writing, and not many copies are to be found outside the Chapel.

Boyle's whole-hearted enjoyment of what he liked was always infectious and inspiring. "That chord is meat and drink to me," was a favourite ejaculation ; as when he might be playing " And in each track of glory " out of Purcell's *Yorkshire Feast Song*. If he was not a *virtuoso*, he

---

[1] Will someone kindly put me on the track of the beautiful tune, "How sweet is the evening air ! " which is possibly in the *Jovial Crew*, but which I cannot now find ?

was extremely skilful at devising accompani-
ments in the grand manner for such compositions
as "Green grow the rushes, O" or the "Emperor
of China" at our orgies. And his parodies of
some of the more saccharine tunes in A. and M.
were worthy not to have been forgotten. Music
was not his only hobby. He was one of the
most accomplished of Dickensians. (Has it
been noticed that a taste for Handel and Dickens
is a frequent blend?) Four of us, Impey,
Childers, Harman and I, once entered for an
examination in *Pickwick* conducted by Boyle,
the winner and examiner to be entertained by
the losers at a breakfast. All was done in order.
The paper was printed, duly headed "King's
College Lecture Room," and a very searching
one it was, more so than that of Calverley. We
repaired at a set time in academical costume to
Boyle's rooms and wrote under his invigilation
for whatever time was allowed. It has always
rankled with me a little that Childers and not I
came out first. But he too was a very careful
student, with an excellent verbal memory.

A great deal of innocent pleasure died with
Boyle, who when he left Cambridge became an
official first in the Local Government Board and
then in the Treasury, and a most useful one.
He was a nephew of the well-known Dean Boyle
of Salisbury, and when in 1888 he married Miss
Curzon of East Dean, the wedding was in the
Cathedral, and all the friends gathered round.

Dr. Mann "officiated" at the organ.   Benson
and Childers were lodged with the Bishop, John
Wordsworth.   The Palace was full of candidates,
for there was an ordination impending.   I
treasure the picture of Childers coming down
rather late to breakfast and finding a book of
devotion being passed round, from which everyone in turn was to read a passage aloud.   Arthur
Benson's account was that he just got through his
piece, but Childers unhappily caught his eye,
and after reading a very few lines in a trembling
voice, impeded by food and hysterics, thrust the
book into the next hand and subsided into his
tea-cup.   He communicated the hysterics to me
shortly after, for I found myself sitting next him
in the nave of the Cathedral, listening to Matins.
The service was Croft in A : beautiful, but as
I took occasion to whisper to Childers, " rather
plaintive."   All *he* said was, " Mrs.   Piper
insisted on calling the deceased the Plaintive."
No two people will agree as to what is funny, we
know : and I am afraid most of my few readers
will not be at home with the quotation.   But
I know it reduced me to helplessness for many
minutes.   Am I deceived, or will the following
extract from a letter of Boyle's amuse others as
it does me ?   It was a time of some public
bereavement, in April 1884.   " Of course we
had the March in *Saul* yesterday—played with
dreadful effect before the anthem. . . . Yesterday
both choir and ante-chapel were crammed with

folks in black : one woman had to be taken out at a very early stage—'just before the Psalms, when people have nothing to do but to look about 'em.' It reminded me a little of the man at the Harrow dinner who was carried out screwed before the soup."

Marcus Dimsdale is another figure of the middle years. As long as he lived in College— before he left it for a very happy family life— he was one of those who were daily met and never without pleasure. The little book *Happy Days*, in which some of his light essays are put together, remains to give a notion of the wholesomeness, the delicacy and fineness of his outlook, and one of the papers (*On Shaving with a Bradshaw*) has more than the rest of his peculiar humour. One feature of this was his delight in playing with words, somewhat in the manner of Lewis Carroll, and also his keen relish for odd and archaic turns of expression, which he would give out with great gusto. One quotation which pleased him was that which recounts the invention of bottled beer, and tells how an angler left his bottle among the rushes, and on coming back to it a day or two later " found no bottle, but a gun." Another from Coryat's *Crudities* was a great favourite. That author, according to Marcus, said that at Padua he had pointed out to him the house of Livy the historian ; and that he credibly believed it might be so, for two special reasons : firstly, because it was indu-

bitably very ancient, and secondly because he
could not bring himself to believe that any
conqueror in any age, however barbarous, would
have destroyed the house of so excellent an
historian and so good a man. This was applied
in many ways. Pointing to a hat (the property
doubtless of a Fellow) hanging outside the Combination Room, Marcus would say : " I credibly
believe that to be the Hat of Livy the historian,
for two reasons : first, because it is indubitably
very ancient " . . . and the rest. Imagination
can readily supply other instances.

Absence of mind was one of his plagues.
Running out one evening from his rooms to post
a letter at the Porter's Lodge, he forgot (like
Churton) the existence of the fountain, and,
less fortunate than Churton, shot straight into it.
A hasty return and a complete change were
necessary before he could achieve his errand.
Of course, he ought, as we told him, to have gone
in at least once more, and allowed some of us to
see : but that was not to be. However, the
incident was of a sort that pleased him very
much in the telling. Of all our company
Walter Headlam was perhaps the most akin
to him in soul. " I loved that man," Marcus
said to me on the day we heard of the death.
Certainly there were many who could truly say
the same of Marcus.

Shall I be blamed for not writing at length of
J. K. Stephen ? I think not. The only time

when he was at all constantly in King's with me
was at the end of his life.   Still, one thing I will
put down, simple of its kind.   He liked his
coffee after lunch, and therefore organised an
institution called the Coffee Club, consisting of
six persons, each of whom was to provide coffee
in his rooms on one week-day—Sunday being a
day of many engagements.   Who were the
original   members ?   J.K.S.,   O.B.,   Marcus
Dimsdale, Wedd, Walter Headlam, myself.   I
think that is right.   The Club lived on for a long
time after J.K.S.'s death, and new members were
co-opted.   It was a genuine tribute that in quite
late days my gyp or bedmaker should have said,
when he or she brought in the coffee, " Poor Mr.
Stephen ! it always reminds me of the Sacrament,
Sir, when I'm doing this."
   In 1884 Walter Headlam and Lionel Ford
were added to our circle.   Of the former—
certain, as I think, had he lived, to have been
the official head of Greek studies in Cambridge,
and, as it was, a prince among scholars—the life
has been written, and I cannot add much to it.
What I do add will be frivolous.   One fine
afternoon George Duckworth arranged that a
party should drive to Audley End.   The party
numbered five :   Walter Headlam and (Sir)
Arthur Hort were of it :   the fifth was Arthur
Goodhart.   Two vehicles, a dog-cart to be
driven by George Duckworth (into which I and
A.M.G. hastily climbed), and a chaise of some

kind, drawn by a yellow pony, stood ready for us
in Trinity Lane. " Will you drive ? " says
Headlam to Hort. " I can't," says Hort. " Well,
nor can I," says Headlam, " but I don't suppose
it's very difficult." Then, to the man in
attendance, " Where's the martingale ? " A
question, he explained afterwards, which he
thought sounded professional. I think he got in
without taking the reins, and I also seem to
recollect that they shot across Trinity Street,
round Rose Crescent, and across the market-
place before they could get into the straight.
But this may be overdoing it. What Hort's
feelings may have been as they started I don't
know ; mine were of deep and selfish thankfulness. We were ahead, and nothing particular
happened until we reached some turning not
very far from Saffron Walden which they ought
to have taken and did not. It was when they
realized this, I fancy, that trouble began. Our
first notice of it was the sound of galloping hoofs
in our rear. The yellow horse was pursuing us,
and fled swiftly past, stimulated by the rattling
of some fragments of shafts attached to the
traces. Filled with apprehension, we turned
back, and soon were much relieved to see two
figures running rather slowly to meet us.
Hort's face was, it is true, drawn with pain, but
Headlam's was calm, though flushed with exer-
tion. It was explained that there had been
some awkwardness about getting the yellow

horse to turn into the right road, the chaise had run up a bank, and Hort had fallen out not only on the point of his hip but also on a tin box of wax matches in his pocket, which had exploded, with their proper effect upon skin and vesture. The pair went sadly on in pursuit of the yellow horse : we drove to the nearest inn to await them, passing the chaise, now reduced to a two-wheeled box, at the side of the road. The chief outcome of this (apart from unfeeling mirth) was a beautiful ode in the manner of Walt Whitman which Headlam read to the Chitchat Society soon after : *A Specimen Day in a Dog-cart.* I am afraid it cannot now be found.

After that, Walter Headlam took to riding, and it became one of the chief pleasures of his life. He had his ambitions once about cricket, but they must have been damped by the character which an unkind Captain wrote for Wisden : " A slow bowler : does not bat or field."

Lionel Ford (should this meet the eye of), he will possibly forgive me for recalling an afternoon we once spent in my rooms on the day of the Boat Procession. This ceremony — long disused — was supposed to be the climax of the May Races. The boats, gaily decked with flowers, and usually manned with anybody but their proper crews, rowed up the Backs to the Mill pool, turned there, and passed down stream. The crowd of May Week visitors and townspeople watched them from the bank, on our back lawn, and our bridge. In the Boats, cups, filled with alcoholic drinks, passed from hand to hand, and most of them found a night's lodging in the river bed, whence they were dredged up next day by the employees of Mr. Millar, from whom they were hired. We of King's rather resented the incursion of the Town over our lawn, and used to watch them with some dislike. On the particular afternoon I am thinking of, Lionel Ford had the lamentable idea of procuring a small looking-glass from my bedroom and *flashing* the crowd on the bank. There was one poor young man who had dressed himself with peculiar care for this occasion, and was looking forward, I doubt not, to an afternoon's enjoyment, and the admiring glances of Sparkling Eyes. Him we picked out (for I cannot deny all complicity) and followed relentlessly : he would plunge into the crowd and be safe for a while, then emerge and angrily glance at our window, only to be brought down by such a well-directed flash as must have made his poor eyes water again. At last he spoke to a policeman ; we saw the officer make a careful reconnaissance, and in no long time heavy steps were to be heard climbing the staircase. However, the door was sported : and the privileges of King's, in regard to the entry of police and even of proctors, are not lightly to be infringed. But, as Thomas Pinch said to Jonas Chuzzlewit, " Was it manly ? Was it kind ? "

I think also that (Dean) Ford's conscience will

not wholly acquit him of having, on another afternoon, taken advantage of the gathering twilight to drop more than one lump of sugar from that same window upon the hat of Dr. Westcott as he passed underneath absorbed in meditation. One hopes that some belated feeling of shame impaired his aim, for it is certain that none of the shots took effect. If memory is not at fault (and if it is, I shall be corrected in a letter to *The Times*), it will have been he also who, in company with Walter Headlam and Sir Walter Raleigh, when the front court was covered with snow, trod out the initials O.B. in colossal proportions, occupying a quarter or more of the lawn. They remained legible for months after the snow had gone. We rather thought Oscar Browning would have appreciated this tribute to his celebrity, but it was not so.

But not all my early associations with Lionel Ford are of this dark complexion. There was much of an uplifting nature in our combined researches into the works of Handel, carried out with the help of a hired piano of great power and, some people said, virulence of tone : the bass part of the compositions being entrusted to Ford, the treble to myself. Here, by the way, is a perplexing incident. Someone, returning to College one still night in summer, told us how he had stood listening—no doubt entranced—to our rendering of " Wretched lovers " (in *Acis and Galatea*) and how the only other sound was the voice of an inmate of Clare College crying out as if in great extremity, " O *do* shut up ! " It may have been a little late, to be sure : there *may* have been something in the *tempo* or the " colour " that he disliked : or perhaps the poor fellow was quite unmusical. We can hardly expect to learn the truth now.

In leaving the subject of these performances, I must be permitted the remark that the rendering of the bass part, particularly in such " numbers " as " Tremble, guilt " (*Susanna*), did not always (*I* should say, only seldom) quite keep pace with the treble.

XVII

IT was in 1883, as I have said, that I made the acquaintance of J. W. Clark over the Greek play, and began to experience that kindness which never failed in all the years that followed. In '84 he flattered me enormously by giving me the proofs of that part of his *Architectural History* which deals with King's and Eton to read, and, as his favourite phrase went, " correct the grosser blunders." That could hardly be done by an undergraduate ; what I learnt from the reading was a new view of the way in which scientific method could be applied to the study of the history of buildings.

It was J.'s uncle, Professor Willis, who, in this country at least, first hit upon the plan, which so strongly appeals to common sense, of getting all possible light both from the building and from the documents about it, and letting the two kinds of evidence play upon each other.

The great work appeared in 1886. The next man who goes over the ground will find very little—in the main lines, nothing—to alter.

Over this we fraternized, and over France, though I never could tolerate Paris, much less love it; in later times, over the history of libraries, but most effectively over common friends. And I was very often at Scroope Terrace and then at Scroope House, places, I can say without any affectation, sanctified in memory by the recollection of Mrs. J.

Everybody who has heard of J., or read of him in Sir Arthur Shipley's book, remembers that he had a great deal of the boy—sometimes the naughty boy—about him. Boyishness was to the fore when you attended a melodrama or a detective play with him, and he filled up all the intervals with guesses, which in spite of his great stage experience were usually wrong, about what was to happen next. Boyish also was his fervid interest in *The Hound of the Baskervilles* when it was coming out in tantalizing monthly instalments in the *Strand.* Sir Arthur Conan Doyle should be gratified if he knew how many evenings were devoted to speculation by under-graduates and others gathered in my rooms, and knew that the numerous false leads he laid down were eagerly followed. J. shared to the full in the excitement. Lady Day came on, when the completed story was to appear in book form, a little before the last instalment in the *Strand.* It was also the day when the University (repre-sented by a few Heads of Houses, officials and professors) assembled by custom in the Provost's Lodge at 11.15 a.m. to partake of coffee and chocolate before proceeding to King's Chapel to hear a sermon. J. and I were both there, and

I had told him that my copy of the *Hound* would be awaiting me in my rooms. We partook of chocolate, and we started from the Lodge door with the procession : but—oh, how it irks me to recall it !—when we reached the corner of the path that turns towards Chapel, J. made me a sign—I fear a preconcerted sign—by laying his wicked old finger on his lips, and we slipped out of the procession and stole up to my rooms : where J., I fancy, was a little disappointed to find that his latest anticipations about the plot were not borne out as they should have been.

I count him to have been naughty on such occasions as the following. The Marlowe Society, which has given so many admirable performances, began its career, as in duty bound, by giving *Dr. Faustus*[1] in the A.D.C. Theatre. I don't suppose J. would ever have taken much stock in *Dr. Faustus*, but, apart from this, no attempt had been made by the Society to enlist his sympathy, for doubtless they were conscious that his dramatic ideals, particularly in the matter of scenery and mounting, were less chastened, less pure, than theirs. So J. was a little prejudiced against the effort. However, Charles Sayle, an earnest devotee, persuaded him to attend a performance, hoping rather against hope, one

---

[1] I have to confess that one outcome of this was the composing of a modernized *Faustus*, adapted to the University conditions of the time, which I was induced to write for a smoking concert at the A.D.C. In some of the blank verse passages I seemed to myself to have captured a faint echo of the Marlowe line.

must suppose, that a convert might be made. I think J. must have felt that he would need some moral support in his Philistine attitude, for he engaged me to be there on the same night, and sit near him. So I did : in the row immediately in front of him and Sayle. Much of the opening scenes was enacted in a subdued light : a practice which J. never could tolerate, but used to describe as " pottering about in the dark." When Rupert Brooke, as Mephistopheles, entered carrying—well, I really don't know what it was —a casket of some kind, J., who was by this time very rebellious, bent over to me and said in a dreadfully audible half-whisper, "What's he bringing in a biscuit-tin for ? " " Hush, J., they'll hear you ! " " No, but I want to *know* what he's bringing in a biscuit-tin for." I could not satisfy him. More enquiries of this kind were wafted to me as the play went on. " Are we not to be permitted to *see* Helen of Troy ? " " Yes, yes, J., there she is." "Oh indeed! fank you : I was not aware of it." Poor Sayle was sadly pained by the profanity, but it is to be feared that J. went away rather elated : as he was on a like occasion when some other injudicious enthusiast took him to see the Irish Players, and he evolved a formula which he repeated to me and many others in the street. " Have you been to see vese Irish Players ? " " No." " Well, I have, and my advice to you is, Don't. It's nuffing more or less van a parcel of incompetent amateurs muttering unintelligible nonsense in ve dark."

Great figures were to be seen in the University in the early eighties: Adams, Cayley, Hort, Kennedy, Munro, Mayor, Seeley, Stokes, Westcott are samples. Cayley was a familiar sight stamping past the back windows of Fellows' Buildings, with the ends of a brown worsted comforter flying behind him : I say stamping, because every few paces he would raise his foot much higher than was necessary—as if to mount a staircase—and bring it down with a slap on the ground : gazing meanwhile into infinity. Stokes, very beautiful to behold, would have been a totally unknown quantity to me but for his kindness in asking me to dinner one night. Probably it was in 1884, when Peterhouse celebrated a sexcentenary and Sir William Thomson (Lord Kelvin) installed electric light in the College. Sir William was at dinner. I sat next to Stokes, who smiled brilliantly but made no kind of attempt to engage me or anyone else in conversation. It somehow happened that I was the last of the party to say good-night. Stokes and Sir William had arranged to go across to Peterhouse and see how the new light was behaving. So I went out with them : and Stokes, as he closed the garden gate behind him, again smiled brilliantly and said in a low but intense voice : " We won't go home till morning." This was the one observation of a frivolous character that I heard from his lips: almost the only one, grave or gay, that I ever heard at all.

I attended, probably in 1885, a course of lectures by J. E. B. Mayor, the Professor of Latin. At the first lecture, perhaps the first and second, I had a companion, Dames Longworth. After that I was alone : alone with Mayor in a small dark room in the Divinity Schools. The thing became a nightmare very soon, but motives of delicacy prevented me from deserting. The subject was the Epistles of Seneca : I have my notes of the lectures still. Each note consists of a Latin word or phrase followed by a long succession of numerals, 108. 12, 254. 17, 303. 2, etc., etc., being, of course, references to other places in Seneca where the word occurred. These notes are the faithful transcript of what was said— except that I have not marked the short coughs with which it was punctuated. There was never any translation, or any explanation of an interesting point. Of course Mayor, imagining that everybody was as conscientious as himself, thought that one would go home and look up all these references and copy out the passages in a neat hand. But !

At the end of the lecture there was an oasis. I used to carry Mayor's books back to his rooms in St. John's, and he would reward me with a copy of the last number of the *Vegetarian Magazine*, or refresh me with the reading of a letter he had written to, or received from, one of the Old Catholic Bishops. Innocency, charity, the purest enthusiasm for learning were seen at their best in Mayor : accompanied by a want of sense of proportion (and humour) which could hardly be exaggerated. I possess a copy of his memoir of his friend Todhunter (of the Euclid) which he began to publish in the *Cambridge Review*: after two or three instalments the editor's patience gave out, and the record had to be printed separately as a book. The scale of it may be judged from the fact that biographies of the Dissenting schoolmasters who taught Todhunter as a boy find a place in it, with careful transcripts of the title-pages of the school-books which they published. Todhunter was Mayor's close friend, but Mayor was only once in his rooms. My experience of this wonderful and lovable old man left me with the impression that he must have sat for the portrait of the Professor or the Other Professor in *Sylvie and Bruno*, perhaps for both.

If the Professor of Latin was remarkable, not less so was Dr. Kennedy, Regius of Greek. With him I very seldom came in contact, except when he examined officially for the University Scholarships. Then he would enter the Senate House with a face like an apoplectic macaw and give out a very prolix notice about the form in which papers were to be shown up. " You will write your names and Colleges at the top of the paper on the right-hand side. Thus, if your name is Jones of Trinity, you will write, on the right-hand side, *Jones*, and below it, *Trinity College*. Or if your name is, etc., etc. You will notice that the paper is divided into five parts, numbered with Roman numerals from I to V. There are five baskets correspondingly numbered on the table, and when you come to give up your answers, each group of answers should be placed in the basket bearing its number. Thus, etc." The sad part was, not only that the necessary directions were already in print on the papers, but that if anyone came in a little late, the whole was recited to him again in a hoarse undertone as he sat at his desk. However, this examination was one of Dr. Kennedy's rare public appearances, and he liked to make the most of it.

I have heard rich descriptions of his demeanour at St. John's, where, during the Twelve Days of Christmas, nightly suppers went on in the Combination Room. Dr. Kennedy enters, and the Steward approaches him, offering a card, that he may make one in a rubber of whist. "No, thank you. I am to preach before the University to-morrow; and it would be very wrong if . . . Well, perhaps just *one* rubber."

The tables are made up. Dr. Kennedy—himself by no means silent—keeps sending messages to the other tables to request that there shall be less talking, and is heard to say in reproachful tones, as if somebody else were to blame : " Of *course*, if I had known that *diamonds* were trumps, I should have played *very* differently." The Steward again approaches, proffering this time some seductive drink. "No, thank you. I am to preach before the University to-morrow, and it would be very . . . Well, perhaps just *one* glass."

But really I have no claim to tell stories about Dr. Kennedy. That should be the care of Salopians.

Will you have another simple tale of a Professor whom I never saw, Pryme, Professor of Political Economy in the 'sixties, a man, as will appear, not very swift at seizing the point ? He was speaking with enthusiasm, and at length, on a favourite topic, his fondness for new port, as opposed to old. Dr. Woodham of Jesus, growing rather restive, broke in on the oration and said : "Well, Pryme, you'd better come and dine with us at Jesus : we're drinking next year's port there now." "Many thanks, Woodham : I shall be very happy," says Pryme, and relapses into thought. The talk of the company passes to other subjects. Then Pryme, suddenly pointing a stiff forefinger at Woodham, says : "But, Dr. Woodham, I do not see how it is *possible* that you should be drinking *next year's* port at Jesus College." This is the only story of Pryme that I can give accurately, to my regret : though I can still hear the crying voice of dear old Dr. Campion of Queen's telling me how Pryme was afflicted with knobs or bubukles on his face, which he thought to cure by a regular diet of Du Barry's Revalenta Arabica, the earliest perhaps of the Patent Foods : whereof the advertisements used to tell us that Pope Pius IX partook every morning, to his great comfort.

Shall we mount the last step in the academic hierarchy? From Professors to Heads of Houses?

I have tried to sketch him of King's. Thompson of Trinity I never spoke to, but quite often on a Sunday evening I have gone to the ante-chapel of Trinity for no other purpose than to see the Master walking up and down there before service began, in a brief surplice, no cassock, and a D.D. hood : and a wonderful sight he was, with his silky white hair and his pallid and—yes, I thought it so—his Satanic face. It was drawn with illness, but very handsome and very formidable.

Dr. Corrie of Jesus I hardly knew by sight. He died at the age of ninety-two, in 1885 : the statement was current among us that his end was hastened by a fall out of an apple-tree, but the very sedate published memoir of the good old man gives no countenance to this. J. had a story about him, possibly inedited. In the middle of the century there had been extensive restorations in Jesus Chapel, and some undergraduates who were in sympathy with the idea of beautifying the place collected funds for the purchase of a new altar cloth, and proceeded to ask an audience of the Master and make their offer. It must have come as a shock to Dr. Corrie, who was a man of markedly anti-tractarian views ; but he received them with great kindness, and only said : " My dear young friends, sin and the Devil have put this idea into your innocent young hearts." I have my doubts as to the complete authenticity of this story : in any case, the memoir I have mentioned gives a very amiable picture of the old gentleman.

Dr. Atkinson of Clare became Master six years before I was born, and continued until the second year in which I was Vice-Chancellor (1856-1915). He was one of the best Latinists of his day : he was also an authority on mediaeval German. I once dined with him, and he talked to me of Bernhard of Regensburg and other such persons. But he was far too humble-minded to think that he could ever publish anything worth reading. He was never seen out of a clerical frock-coat and top-hat: no, not even when he took his summer holiday at Hunstanton, and the unkind wind blew his hat into the sea, and he would have had to return to Mrs. Atkinson bareheaded, had not some young men who were indulging in "a game called golf" charitably lent him a cloth cap. This was, I take it, one of the most vivid adventures of his later years.

When the University went in state to Clare College to congratulate the Master on attaining his Jubilee (in 1906), I know that the opening words of his reply were " Acute conscius sum "

—" I am acutely conscious "—and I have often wondered whether this extreme literality was a mark of superlatively good Latin, or—not.

The accession of Ben Latham to Trinity Hall is near enough to the point I have reached. He succeeded Sir Henry Maine in 1888. But I did not see much of him before I joined the " Family," of which anon.

To hear Latham talk you would imagine he cared for nothing but stocks and shares, or curious wines, or rowing. But read the two or three books he published, *Pastor Pastorum*, *The Risen Master*, *A Service of Angels*, and your idea of him will be strongly infused with reverence. He was much interested, too, in Shakespeare : one day in the street he told me of a convincing emendation of the old crux in Hamlet, the *dram of eale*, which he had just hit upon. What was it ? Ah, there you have me. I only know that at the time I thought it was very good !

The stories of his ravens, of his widow-proof room, and the rest, are sure to have been chronicled. If they have not, it is clearly the duty of a pious member of Trinity Hall to write them down. He had a sort of quite simple humour which his deliberate utterance used to invest with a charm that deserts the written word. He quoted to me the instance of a Trinity Hall man who suffered in the Marian persecution, and added, seemingly with some sense of injury, " Now, you know, if *I* was to burn one of *my* undergraduates alive in the front court, I should never hear the last of it." I laughed consumedly, but who knows if a reader will even smile ?

A fair number of the Heads who were in office when I came up belonged to the generation who regarded themselves and their Order with extreme reverence. It is on record, perhaps in several places, how a Head's wife said to the wife of a Professor who had just become a Head : " Of course, dear, we shall be able to see much more of each other, now you have become one of Us." I do not think I ever took quite that view of them, even in the earliest days. The majority of those whom I have not dealt with particularly were rather dim old gentlemen. Phillips of Queen's, Swainson of Christ's, Phelps of Sidney, Worsley of Downing, these seemed primaeval ; and others who had really been in office for quite a short time, such as Ferrers of Caius, Searle of Pembroke, Phear of Emmanuel, appeared just as old and crusted. But enough of the Heads : I will resist the temptation of trying to set down, what Henry Jackson often told me, the true history of " Robinson's Vote," *i.e.* the vote given by Dr. Robinson for himself in 1861, which made him Master of St. Catharine's for forty-eight years. I am not sure enough of the details to venture on the story. All I *am* sure of is that he was a very ill-used man, and that the ostracism he suffered for years at the hands of the University was quite unmerited.

XVIII

So, back to 1885. The Easter vacation of that year I spent at the Tancred Arms in the village of Hawnby near Helmsley with Arthur Benson, Tatham, T. W. Little, and (part of the time) Inge. We read for our several Triposes and paid particular attention to the songs sung of an evening in the bar by the blacksmith and others. Many of them I retain *verbatim*. One offers a curious corruption. It was about a Yorkshireman who " went up to London a few weeks ago " and successfully eluded the efforts of the Cockneys to get the better of him. The chorus ran thus :

> But ah ! (says I)
> Wait till Good Friday Whit Monday fall,
> Wait till there's priests to the make of St. Paul,
> Wait till Cornelius or Roger set free
> And then you may reckon of didd-e-ling me.

Line 3 puzzled me for some time till I excogitated the true reading : Wait till Kenealy Sir Roger set free. Whence we see that the Lay in its present form is not very ancient, the Tichborne Trial having only ended in 1874.

What about the following ballad ? It was sung by the blacksmith to the melody of " The First Good Joy that Mary had," and it is evidently akin to one that begins : " John Wesley had a little ghost." Is the following version known ?

> Why do these Bugs torment me so ?
> I never did them any 'arm ;
> They comes to me when I'm asleep
> By thousands in a swarm.
>> By thousands in a swar-haw-hawm,
>> By thousands in a swar-haw-hawm,
>> They comes to me when I'm asleep
>> By thousands in a swarm.

> There is one Bug amongst this lot,
> His name it is Big Joe ;
> He's got two rows of fostle teeth
> All on his bottom jaw-r.
>> All on his . . . etc.

> My father's got a bantam cock,
> My mother's got an 'en,
> My sister's got some barley-corns
> To feed them now hand then.
>> To feed . . . etc.

> My father's got a bran-new coat,
> My mother's got a gown,
> My sister said she'd 'ave the same,
> My father he knocked her down.
>> My father . . . etc.

It seems impossible with the resources at hand to divine what led the minstrel either to the choice of his subject or to the abrupt change of mood in the third stanza.

I also retain in memory a quatrain printed on a mourning-card in one of the bedrooms. I have no other knowledge of the incident it records :

No one to help them, no one to save,
No one but Heaven to point out their grave !
The poor man and his son, who had done him no harm,
Were murdered by Charters at Cropton Lane Farm.

It was mainly to preserve these lyrics—a mere
fraction of what I might have inflicted—that I
have made any mention of holiday pursuits.
There is no intention of doing that regularly, nor
any undertaking not to do it at all. In fact, I
have now reached a time when—the framework of
Cambridge life having been described to the best
of my ability—large tracts can be passed over very
lightly. I record that in the thirty-six years from
1882 to 1918 there were only two Cambridge
terms which I did not keep by residence. The
first was the Lent term of 1886, which I spent at
Eton, taking the division of a Master who was
ill. It was my lot to impart instruction to R. C.
Norman, Chairman of the L.C.C., to General
Mott, and other eminent persons, and I enjoyed
it, but did not feel a vocation to the teaching
profession.

The other term I missed was the Lent
term of '88, for in the winter of '87 I went out
on an archæological mission to Cyprus and had
my first and only experience of excavating work
in company with D. G. Hogarth and Ernest
Gardner. The principal site we had to deal with
was the temple of Aphrodite at Paphos. It would
be cruel to unload on these pages details which
have been chronicled in their proper places, but

I must make my tribute to our foreman and guide
Gregorio. He had been associated with General
Cesnola's sporadic and rather mischievous excavations in the island, and had developed
uncanny instincts for such work. He could
neither read nor write, nor speak any English,
but he would be greatly excited when an inscription in the Cypriote syllabary turned up, and had
a very just appreciation of the quality of the
small objects that were found. But what used
to surprise me most was his unerring knowledge
of the quality of soil. You would walk with him
over a rough field, and from time to time he
would plunge a long iron rod with a point, which
he always carried, into the ground. It brought up
a little earth on the end. Gregorio would rub
this between his finger and thumb and pronounce
either that it was καϊάσ—virgin earth—or made
soil. In the latter case he would study the surface
of the ground and perhaps in the end point to a
shallow depression and say it was worth a trial.
He was always right. A couple of men with
spades would very quickly uncover the beginning
of a flight of steps cut in the rock (which was
everywhere very near the surface) and you would
speedily find yourself entering a series of rock-
cut chambers. Probably you would find that
they had been rifled, but they were still full of
pottery, and masses of eggs (provender for the
dead), and often remains of rather cheap wreaths
of thin gold leaves. Gregorio's lack of English

was a very valuable thing to me, for it necessitated my learning to talk Greek. I used to make him tell me παραμυθίασ—fairy tales—and gradually absorb the drift of them. As you are aware, in most tales the same thing happens three times. In our hurried age we are content to state this, but if the tale is rightly told, each occurrence must be repeated, in the same words, at full length. The consequence was that a story might beguile a ride of three hours, and also that you might hope from the second or third repetition of an episode to keep pace with what was going on. The longest of all the stories was the one about a prince promised to a magician (a δράκος) before his birth, in which is a quest for the water of Life, and two cowardly princes who allow the hero to brand them on condition that he gives them the water which he has been at the expense and trouble of getting himself. It is a well-known saga.

I have the brightest recollections of Cyprus. Life was made all the pleasanter because I had a brother in the R.A.M.C. quartered there : and Sir Charles Warren and the English residents generally were very kind. We coincided with Professor Sayce : also with W. H. Mallock, who was gathering materials for a book—in which I pass across one of the pages, under a fancy name, which I have forgotten, along with the name of the book itself. But the wonderful mixed flavour of the island is what I should dearly like to experience again: the compound of a kind of Hellenic civilization with three or four later ones —ancient Greek inscriptions built up into cottage walls, Burgundian Gothic churches, a Turkish bath paved with tombstones of French knights, beautifully carved Venetian pulpits in the churches, beautiful minarets rising out of fourteenth century Gothic towers, hideous little Greek churches with more hideous wall paintings. The Cathedral of Nicosia is typical, where you enter beneath a triple porch like that of Notre Dame at Dijon, and find a whitewashed interior with all the prayer carpets on the floor pointing crookedly to the south-east, the mihrab that marks the direction of Mecca being several degrees out of the main axis of the building. But to my lasting regret, some of the best things in Cyprus I was unable to see—the ruined Abbey of Bella Pais and the Cathedral of Famagusta.

XIX

THE task of selection of experiences is now becoming really difficult. All these years were of course full of interest to me, but how is it to be supposed that I can impart any glimmer of the light that rests on them to anyone else ?

Let me be even more egotistical than I have been, and write for a space about my work. A Bachelor's degree had been duly taken in 1885. I was more free now to look about and scent out a subject or subjects which should interest me. At no time had I thought systematically about a career, I am afraid ; but this much was plain, that if I wanted to make King's my headquarters I must do my best to obtain a Fellowship. The road to this was the writing of a dissertation : and to me the obvious department to look for a subject was among the Apocryphal writings. I had cherished for years, I still cherish, a quite peculiar interest in any document that has claimed to be a Book of the Bible, and is not. Nowadays I suppose it would be proper to say that I have a complex about it. A dream of my childhood is still vivid to me, in which I opened a folio Bible in a shiny black binding, and found in it a Book of about the length of Obadiah, occupying a single page, divided into verses and with a heading in italics, all quite ship-shape. It was called (I think) the *Book of Maher-shalal-hash-baz*. At least the name was a long Hebrew one beginning with M. And for years after I hoped I might some day come on the real thing, and whenever a chance offered I read with avidity anything that was classed as apocryphal, and wrote down careful abstracts of it in note-books. With what joy I carted off from the circulating library at Bury and carried for several miles the eighth volume, in folio, of De la Bigne's *Bibliotheca Patrum*, which contains Latin versions of the Testaments of the Twelve Patriarchs and more such matter ! The day on which a kind clerical friend lent me that very bad book, Hone's *Apocryphal New Testament*, was another white one. But when I was able, on my way back to Eton, to buy for sixteen shillings the four classical volumes of John Albert Fabricius on the Apocrypha of both Testaments (from the friendly bookseller John Mozley Stark of King William Street, Strand), life appeared to have little more to offer. I bless in parenthesis the memory of Mr. Stark, who let me look at his best books and MSS unhindered, and *gave* me leaves of MSS taken out of bindings, which were of the greatest help to me in learning to read and copy old hands. Mr. Stewart, too, whose shop was next door, and who was a specialist in occult literature, showed me Barrett's *Magus* and other

classics of wizardry which made a deep impression.   I see, however, that I am diving back into
the seventies. . . . . Well, the dissertation, I
settled, should be on the subject of the apocryphal
Apocalypse of St. Peter, which had enjoyed a
great reputation in the second century, but of
which, as it happened, only about half a dozen
lines survived, in quotations.   Those six lines,
however, contained enough clues to suggest what
the subject of the book had been : and I wove
about them a web of considerable size.   A few
years later a large piece of the text, found in
Egypt in 1884, was printed, and served to confirm
my main guesses or conclusions, while of course
it put others of them out of court.   Side by
side with this I was reading all the catalogues
of manuscripts I could find, in the hope of
stumbling on some unnoticed text in my line
of business.   I thought one day that I could
trace, lurking in the Bodleian Library under a
misleading title, the complete Greek text of the
romance of Joseph and his wife Asenath, a very
pretty story known to exist in Syriac and Latin,
but of which only a bit of the Greek was in print
—this bit, by the way, having been edited from
the very MS that stood next on the shelf to mine.
I went off at once to Oxford, was introduced to
the Bodleian by Professor Chandler (a unique
distinction, I may say), and found my hopes
realized.   The text was speedily copied out.   Then
I heard that a French scholar, Abbé (now Mon-

signor) P. Batiffol, was engaged on an edition of
the book from Greek MSS in the Vatican: so on
Dr. Hort's advice I sent him my transcript and
also a new and fuller Latin version which I had
found at Corpus Christi, and that was the pro-
pitious beginning of acquaintance with foreign
scholars. It was also the beginning of quite a
number of other finds due to the same simple
process of reading catalogues. The Testament of
Abraham was found to be accessible at Oxford.
Later on, a piece of a Latin version of the Book
of Enoch turned up in the British Museum, and,
best of all, a large and deeply heretical fragment
of the Acts of St. John at Vienna : and so on.
Apocrypha, then, was one rewarding hobby.

I was elected to a Fellowship in March of
1887. Besides this, Dr. Waldstein had offered
me a post under him in '86, as Assistant Director
of the Fitzwilliam Museum, where I was able
not only to keep up an interest in Classical
Archaeology, but also to go on describing on an
extended scale the illuminated MSS that form part
of Lord Fitzwilliam's magnificent bequest. Needless to say, one learnt a great deal from the
process of describing every single picture in
some 130 MSS. So fascinating was the employ-
ment that I determined I would extend it to
other Cambridge libraries. Nor was it long
before I realized that the survey, if it was to be
really useful, must include *all* the mediaeval
MSS, not only those that had pictures ; so that

before long I was making bargains with kind and long-suffering Colleges, that if they would print catalogues of their MSS I would make those catalogues. The result has been a row of seventeen or eighteen Cambridge catalogues, besides others done for Eton, Westminster Abbey, the Rylands Library, and Messrs. H. Yates Thompson and Pierpont Morgan: *and*, one of the stoutest of all, *which still remains in manuscript*, that of the mediaeval MSS at Lambeth.

I have glided insensibly into talk about manuscripts. Perhaps some kind of coherence, sadly wanting in these pages, will result from my now putting together some of the less unreadable results of years spent in foraging among them. I have had to handle so many collections of quite miscellaneous volumes that I have been distracted from specializing on any one class or period, and though I imagine myself able to date most books correctly enough, I cannot and never could cultivate the sort of brain and eye, such as Jenkinson possessed in a marvellous degree, which carries in it the special form of the letter g (say) and can tell you with certainty that it does not occur after the year 850. The fact is that since I began to busy myself with these things, the department of learning called palaeography has been more and more justifying its claim to be called an exact science. The multiplication of photographic facsimiles enables a student to have under his eye all the extant examples of

writing of a given date. The methods of abbre-
viation and contraction of words that were in
use in different *scriptoria* and different countries
have been studied and classified. The scripts
of Corbie, Laon, Reichenau, Lyons, and several
other great centres are known entities. As
time goes on, we shall be able to differentiate
yet more minutely. What applies to writing is
true of illumination as well. The younger
workers in the field can look forward to dis-
criminating the ateliers at which miniaturists
worked in France or England in a way which was
not dreamt of thirty years ago. I follow their
advance with interest and pleasure, but cannot
emulate them. If I have had a part to play, it
has been that of making known, with what
fulness of description I could, the existence of
a mass of material, and assigning dates and
provenances which in the main are, I hope,
correct. But I have had to learn my job as I
went on : my catalogues were on a scale that
had not been tried before, and the later ones
compare (in my judgment) favourably with the
earlier, which I could now improve in many
respects.

This work, which may not unfairly be called
superficial, or at least preliminary, has been a
great solace. It has resulted in the accumulation
of a heap of scraps of odd miscellaneous information, scraps which often enough are found
to be really threads connecting one book with

another, and perhaps in the end helping to link up a whole group, and reveal a whole chapter in the history of a library. One heap of scraps is composed of the press-marks which various English monasteries wrote on the fly-leaves of their books. At some one moment I recognized the special form of the Bury St. Edmund's press-mark. My home was within six miles of Bury. The Abbey Gate and the Norman Tower were most familiar objects. It seemed a fit tribute to local patriotism to try to gather what could be found out—first about the Library. I cannot remember who or what made me aware of the fact that at Pembroke College there were some MSS from Bury. There is in fact a great block of them, given in 1599 by an Ipswich alderman, William Smart. This nucleus secured, it remained to be seen what the British Museum and other collections contained. Something led me to the Arundel MSS at the Heralds' College, and there I found a Bury book in which an owner had written down a large number of verses inscribed on windows and paintings in the Abbey church. All this was new information, and suggested the gathering of knowledge about the buildings as well as the Library. It seemed likely, next, that there might be something to be found at Douai : some few MSS from the English Benedictine College, as the catalogue showed, were in the Town Library. A dash thither followed, and was rewarded by the sight not only of the Douai Psalter, but of a Bury register which revealed the sites of the tombs of the early abbots, including Abbot Samson (verified by subsequent excavations). The Douai Psalter I may count myself fortunate to have seen and taken notes of. It was the most beautiful of a group of Psalters belonging to the years about 1300, executed somewhere in East Anglia. Whether it belonged, as I thought, to an Abbot of Bury, is now questioned : anyhow, it was a lovely thing. In the early days of the War, when the Germans were approaching Douai, it was placed in a tin case and buried in the near neighbourhood of the Library. I am told that it was not buried deep enough, and that heavy lorries drove over the spot and so crushed the metal case that water got in. When it was dug up after the War, it was a wet unopenable lump of vellum, and so it is like to remain. That is the account I have heard. I need add no comment.

So one thing leads to another, and so it was that materials enough about Bury Library and the Abbey Church were collected to fill an octavo volume. But if you interest yourself in one library, why not, as you go on, note what you can about others ? Canterbury MSS were always turning up : I began to discriminate between those of Christchurch (the Cathedral) and of St. Augustine's Abbey. A Christchurch script was identified by the help of MSS at Trinity. The kind and patient attendants in the MS room at the British Museum were long kept busy with hauling trucks full of heavy books to my seat that they might be examined in search of press-marks. To be as little tedious as possible, a fat book on the ancient libraries of Canterbury and Dover came out in 1904. Thus, the reconstruction of extinct libraries became a by-product of the cataloguing of MSS.

The chase of the manuscript and the publication of results was likely to bring me across the path of scholars abroad as well as at home. So were researches among the apocryphal literature : so, too, the connexion with the Fitzwilliam Museum. Paul Meyer, who had first come over to England at the time of the war of 1870, had made a speciality, then and after, of searching English libraries for French MSS : he was always most ready to give help about those at Cambridge. Léopold Delisle I saw but once, at Paris, not long before he died, though we exchanged letters fairly often. He seemed to be the ideal of the learned Frenchman. I could not wonder that he was adored by the younger savants for his personality as well as for the immense range of his knowledge and the finish and beauty of his work. But with Samuel Berger, the Protestant theologian and antiquary, I was on more familiar terms. He was a merry man, full of songs which hailed from his native Alsace. One which is printed in *Mélusine* (a French folk-lore periodical) was a special favourite :

" De Saint Joseph un jour c'était la fête,
Tout le Paradis se mit en tête de danser :
' Moi,' dit Joseph, ' je ne suis pas si bête,
J'ai bien autre chose à penser.
Bon pour Cath'rine et pour Nicolas,
Mais je n' dans'rai pas, car je suis trop las.
Danse, Nicolas, si de danser est ton envie,
Danse, Nicolas, pour moi je n' dans'rai pas '."

In fact, St. Joseph was very disagreeable about
it—on his birthday, too !—and resisted the blan-
dishments of several Saints : but in the last
verse the Virgin succeeded in clearing his brow,
and making him take the floor with her. Songs
like this were warbled by Berger—and very well
too—as he walked the streets of Paris, and
showed R. C. Norman and me the basilica of
S. Denis and the glass of Montmorency. Everybody was fond of him.

He had been a pupil of Duchesne and continued
to be a great friend. The two of them came to
Cambridge in 1894 to receive honorary degrees,
and much enjoyed being photographed in their
robes. Duchesne, who was then writing or
about to write something bearing on the validity
of English Orders, but who was on this occasion
out to enjoy himself, exercised a good deal of
ingenuity in the effort, not always successful,
to elude certain worthy enthusiasts on that
subject who lay in wait to nobble him.

Wilamowitz was the greatest foreign classic
whom I had the honour of receiving, in 1908, when
he too came for an honorary degree, and may

have been a good deal puzzled by the May Races to which I took him, introducing him to Walter Headlam there.   It was but a few days later that Headlam died, and Wilamowitz sent me some beautiful Greek elegiacs in memory of him.

Now let me chronicle one of the few lucky finds of MSS which fell to my share.   In or about 1700 a Mr. Edward Colman bequeathed a library to the parish of Brent Eleigh in Suffolk.   It contained some nine MSS.   In 1887 the parish authorities, needing funds for some purpose, put two of them into a sale in London.   One was a late Martial, the other was a little book of the Gospels.   The latter was bought for the Bodleian for about nine pounds.   It turned out to be the very Gospel-book once owned by Queen St. Margaret of Scotland, mentioned in her Life as the subject of a miraculous rescue when it had fallen into the water.   The provenance of it was not made public at the time, so no further curiosity about the Brent Eleigh Library was excited.   In 1890 an old friend, F. R. Chapman, Archdeacon of Sudbury, told me there were still some MSS at Brent Eleigh, so, as soon as I could, I went over to see them, and found them housed in a small dank building in the churchyard.   I was allowed to take some or all of them back to Cambridge for examination.   After a rapid negotiation they all became the property either of the University Library or the Fitzwilliam in 1891, soon after which the whole library was dispersed. None of the MSS was without interest, but two were unique—a volume containing the long-lost life of St. William of Norwich (a boy supposed to have been kidnapped and crucified by Jews in 1124) and a bulky but mutilated *Register of British Saints*, written in the early part of the seventeenth century by Nicolas Roscarrock—it has formed a mine of information to hagiologists. The St. William was a considerable find, for it is the oldest of a long series of tales of boys slain by the Jews. Upon consideration, I thought that Dr. Jessopp would be the right person to handle a monument of Norwich history of this importance. The correspondence I began with him ended in a collaboration : we brought out the Life in 1896. The resulting friendship with Dr. Jessopp and the visits to Scarning were handsome rewards for any weariness entailed by the translation (which I still think I did rather well) of the miracles of St. William out of the distressing Latin of Thomas of Monmouth, who recorded them. One of my visits to Dr. Jessopp included an afternoon of great interest to me. He took me to Norwich and introduced me to the late Professor Knapp, who was then living in the city and working at his life of George Borrow. Being a devotee of that author, I was glad to sit for three or four hours and have a flood of information poured over me. It was punctuated in a curious way : every few minutes Professor Knapp's enthusiasm over-

came him and he gave vent to two or three sobs :
" O, he *was* a good man ! " he would say, and
then dry his eyes, and go on. He had got
together the most surprising collection of documents about Borrow—proof-sheets of *Lavengro*
(then called *Life*), coach-bills of coaches by
which Borrow had travelled from Norwich to
London, above all the household account-books
which Borrow had kept for his mother (who
could not write) at a time when Borrow rather
wished it to be understood (in after years) that
he had been roaming over the interior of Asia.
He had penetrated, too, most of the masks
under which Borrow conceals the identities of
the people he meets: some of these he said he
could not divulge to the public : probably all
have leaked out by this time.

Other purchases made about this time for the
Fitzwilliam might also be reckoned now as
lucky, but chiefly in view of the terrific inflation
of prices which has supervened since they were
made. Still, I shall always think the Carew-
Poyntz Hours a cheap book at £120. It is a
fourteenth century English Book of Hours, very
full indeed of pictures—not of the first style,
but very lively and uncommon. Among them
is a set of illustrations of the Miracles of the
Virgin which was of great use in helping me to
interpret the broken sculptures of the Lady
Chapel at Ely. In that lovely building, each
division of the arcade that runs round the lower

stage has two bas-reliefs. The softness of the clunch in which they are carved has made it an easy and congenial task for some adherent of the Protector (perhaps) to walk round, stick in hand, and knock off all the heads and as much of the bodies of the figures as might happen to follow. Except for the obvious guess that these sculptures must have illustrated the story of the Virgin in some way, nobody had tried his hand at deciphering them. They constituted a puzzle of the kind dear to my heart, and I had not pored over them very long before I saw that one certainly represented the Presentation of the Virgin in the Temple. Working backwards and forwards from this fixed point, I was able to " get the hang " of the whole series and embody the results in a paper read to the Archaeological Association in 1892. Bishop Lord Alwyne Compton then interested himself in the matter, munificently paid for the photographing of every bay (which entailed the temporary removal and the rebuilding of the organ), and arranged for the publication of a fine quarto on the subject.

Other decipherments of sculptures—of the bosses in the Cloisters of Norwich Cathedral and in the Bauchun Chapel there—followed. This work gave me a delightful acquaintance in Chancellor Bensly.

XX

BUT, as Mr. Smangle said, "This is dry work."
Let us get back to the human element. Among
the new figures who came on the scene, or of
whose existence I became aware, John Henry
Middleton was one. He joined the College in
1886, on his election to the Slade Professorship
of Fine Art, and speedily made himself a niche in
our affections. Clad in a dressing-gown or a
velveteen coat, and a skull-cap, and smoking a
kind of shag (as I should call it) named "Golden
Returns," he sat and retailed in a level voice,
with frequent slight dramatic pauses, the most
startling personal experiences. The puzzled
hearers would at times compare notes of dates and
places, and try vainly to construct a chronological
table of Middleton's career. He had seen Bomba
arrive, fleeing for refuge, at the Italian convent
where he was at school : he remembered well
the promulgation of the Dogma of the
Immaculate Conception. He had fished for
alms out of the window of a prison at Aleppo,
had had an audience of the Sultan at Fez,
advancing with some trepidation along the hall
to where the Sultan sat flanked by two live lions
—unattached : had slept or not slept in the

native home of the bed-bug (in a Central American forest) : had seen, on the broad and boundless Perearers, Apaches transfix American soldiers with arrows shot from horseback : had also seen a performance of the celebrated rope-trick.   This, for I remember it very well, I will set down as he told it.   He was walking out with a friend in the neighbourhood of (Algiers ? Tunis ? anyhow, in North Africa) in the sandy desert.   There met them a naked man with a coil of rope loosely hung on one arm, who greeted them and asked if they would like to see a trick. Being bidden to proceed, he took the coil of rope from his arm and so threw it that it uncoiled upwards to its full length.   It then remained hanging vertically in the air like a bell-rope, with the lower end a foot or two off the ground.   The wizard stood away from it and invited them to pull it.   When they did so, it yielded much as a bell-rope does ; when they let go, it moved up again to its former position.   They signified that they had seen enough.   The wizard gave the rope a jerk and it fell down on the ground : he coiled it up, hung it on his arm again, received his fee, and walked off.   There was no talk of his climbing up the rope and vanishing at the top.   Well, there you are : that is a very accurate report.

Another of his conjuring-trick stories was of a performance at San Francisco by a Chinaman. The company were assembled in a carpeted drawing-room. The conjurer cleared the whole centre of the room and laid down a cloth over the carpet—perfectly flat. The spectators were made to stand on the edge of it all round. I suppose incantations came next. Presently beneath the centre of the cloth there appeared a very slight swelling, which grew and grew till it became (say) two feet long, and then began to stir and move. The Chinaman took up the cloth and revealed a live naked baby, which he took away with him.

Besides having been seemingly in every part of the world and done and suffered every conceivable thing, Middleton was much at home in Oxford and London circles. He had been at Exeter College. I remember with satisfaction his story of a freshman from the wilds who for some time succeeded in going every day to *both* of the dinners in Hall, and was only detected in the end because he was heard to murmur to himself (on reading the menu), " Roast turkey and plum pudding *twice* in one day ! This is indeed a treat ! " In town he had been intimate with the great pre-Raphaelites, and, he said, followed them in considering *Our Mutual Friend* to be by far the greatest of Dickens's novels. " Don't sauce *me* in the vicious pride of your youth " may be recognized, by some of the circle who knew him, as a favourite catch-word. If you do not know who said it, you have but to read *Our Mutual Friend*.

The beautiful order and neatness of all his work—plans, drawings, notes—was a Moral. And it may be imagined that with all his store of learning and romance he was a most choice companion. He took me once to his home at Cheltenham (where he had practised as an architect), and often did I explore Suffolk and Cambs. with him. He continued me as his Assistant Director when he succeeded Dr. Waldstein at the Fitzwilliam, and when he left in '93 for South Kensington, I took his place. London did not suit him nearly so well as King's, where he was very happy, and he died, alas! in '96.

When he left Cambridge I moved into his rooms at the top of Wilkins's Building, facing the south door of the Chapel.

Robertson Smith, Arabic Professor, and, after 1886, University Librarian, was another great personage. The circle at Christ's, where he was a Fellow, included other friends of mine, Armitage Robinson, for instance, and Arthur Shipley. Robertson Smith came much nearer to taking all knowledge for his province than anyone else I have met. Had he not edited the *Encyclopaedia Britannica*, and was he not competent to correct the proofs of the mathematical articles therein ? Have I not heard him quoting Persian poetry (unless it was Arabic) by the yard, capping E. G. Browne ? Did he not offer to collaborate with me in a large work on the subject of *Dragons*? Shipley, who tended him so filially in his last illness, has written of his lovableness and bravery, but I too should like to bear my witness to it. Never had anybody better right to pose as a savant, never was anybody further from any kind of pose. An evening with the circle at Christ's (and the '47 port) was—well, there are a great many *clichés* that could be used—let me spare you and say it was *exceedingly pleasant*.

When work among the Trinity M⁵S began, I was brought in contact with Aldis Wright, Librarian and Vice-Master. In his frock-coat, with his beautiful head of white hair, and his white whiskers, and regarding you with intense severity, his outer man did not at once invite familiarity. All the same, I would ask no better than to be his neighbour at dinner or in the Combination Room. I will not say that his austere features melted into smiles, because they did not; but he could be very lively over murders, or the quotations in Burton's *Anatomy*, or some other of the subjects of which he was a master. He was an ardent East Anglian (he had a house at Beccles) and thawed perceptibly on finding me also to be a denizen. " What's a dutfen ? " seemed to be a test question, which I believe I passed with credit. After a very few meetings there was no question of thawing : I even ventured sometimes on an approach to pulling his leg, by asking with every appearance of interest whether it was not the fact that he had now declared himself a convert to the Shakespeare-Bacon theory. This mild pleasantry (repeated at judicious intervals) was always very repaying, for he was not quite certain whether I was serious, and would meet my eye with a terrific glare ; but a rich laughter and a rich invective generally followed. I have had the happiness, when I went to his rooms late in the evening, of finding him at his desk wrapped in a Scotch plaid and with a Tam o' Shanter on his head. Perhaps the impression I give here is that I feared Aldis Wright more than I liked him : exactly the reverse is the case : I was very fond of him. The worst offence I ever committed in his eyes was to ride a bicycle along the Coton path, when he was walking there. His face was corrugated with passion, but he said no word.

On the same landing in Nevile's Court lived, of course, Henry Jackson, than whom King's, Old and New, had no more faithful friend : than whom no one nearer to one's idea of Dr. Johnson will be seen. Year after year he was the guest of Nixon at our Founder's feast, and it was a regular feature of the evening that he should go at a late hour to the orgy called the Junior Combi and make a speech, in which he always paid the most cordial of tributes to the College as he had known it both in earlier and later days. One of the numerous omissions of my undergraduate days was that I never went to his lectures. The truth is, I thought I should make nothing of them : if I meant that I could never have really assimilated Greek philosophy, I was right. The enjoyment of Henry Jackson's company, however, was entirely independent of his eminence in any branch of knowledge. At one time and another I had much of it. For example : something put him on the track of *Edwin Drood* (must I say that this is Dickens's unfinished novel ?) : I think it was the fact (which I can't account for) that I began writing about it in the *Cambridge Review*. Jackson considered it to be the best thing Dickens ever wrote (except, of course, *Pickwick*) : he valued construction in a novel, and this is certainly Dickens's most careful plot, but the view is to me preposterous. Anyhow, Jackson plunged into the Drood question. Anstey Guthrie told him the MS was at South Kensington : he went there, examined it with the scholar's eye, found out some very telling things about it, and wrote a book (*About Edwin Drood*, 1911) which is a really original contribution to the controversy. Six of us, calling ourselves the *Edwin Drood Syndicate*, went down early in July of 1909 to Rochester to examine the possibilities of various theories on the spot—*e.g.* What access was there to the crypt ? Was there anything answering to the Sapsea monument ? What were the relative positions of the Vineyard, Durdles's yard,

Minor Canon Corner ? etc.—and a very memorable week-end we spent there, conducted about by Mr. Edwin Harris, an ardent Dickensian of the city. We attained clearness on some points, but did not hit on any illuminating facts. ' We ' were Jackson, Shipley, H. H. Brindley of St. John's, F. A. Potts of Trinity Hall, and Dickens (a grandson), also of Trinity Hall, an undergraduate and a very pleasant component of the party, and self. Mr. Harris, I will record, told us how he had the same experience when he was a child that befel Peepy Jellyby in *Bleak House ;* for he put his head between the balusters of Rochester Bridge and couldn't get it back. The crowd that collected was helpless too : but Charles Dickens himself, walking into town from Gad's Hill, came to the rescue, and released him.

Like Dr. Johnson, Henry Jackson was a " tremendous companion," but not because he thundered and lightened on slight provocation. He did indeed look at you ταυρηδόν, bull-like, from under his eyebrows, until he had gathered what you meant. Nor would he let loose statements pass : you had to be sure what you did mean and that it was something coherent, or you had better not try to say it. But there was no trampling on the defenceless—I don't, by the way, accuse Dr. Johnson of that—and there *was* every quality of strong sterling virtue that we admire in the old hero.

The name of Jackson calls up that of Henry

Sidgwick, his colleague in so many projects of University reform. I had but few meetings with him, but at one of them he made a critical remark which I think worth preserving. He said that there was a stanza in Praed's poems which seemed to him supremely successful in mingling humour with pathos :

> " Wild Nick was wont to blacken eyes
> Without the fear of sessions ;
> Charles Medlar loathed false quantities
> As much as false professions :
> Now Nick keeps order in the land,
> A magistrate pedantic ;
> *And Medlar's feet repose unscanned*
> *Beneath the wide Atlantic.*"

And Henry Sidgwick's name calls up that of James Ward : externally just the typical philosopher, apt to make you think that there was something to be said for the immortal Mr. Edwards's view (in Boswell), " I have tried too in my time to be a philosopher : but, I don't know how, cheerfulness was always breaking in."

XXI

Now having written of some—not nearly all—
of the elder people whom I had reason to love or
respect, or both, I will try, what is more difficult,
to commemorate some of the younger who are
not here any more.

In 1893 James McBryde came from Shrewsbury to King's ; only succeeding, as he insisted,
in passing the Entrance Examination because
the Mathematical paper set him happened to
be one of the sample ones that he had been
made to do, in preparation for the test, at
Shrewsbury. This accident, deplorable from
some points of view, was, we found reason to
think, a very lucky one. McB. made his way
into our hearts by mere natural goodness. In
person he was not tall, had light curly hair, and
a kind smile : in short, conciliated goodwill.
Before long he formed the habit, which I
always encouraged, of dropping in uninvited at
a late hour of the evening, and joining a congregation which was usually to be found in the
inner room. Here he would be drawn out by
Arthur Jelf, who had in a high degree the faculty
of asking intelligent questions with every mark
of the deepest sincerity and interest and rocking

with inward mirth at the answers he received :
but the mirth was not at McB.'s expense : it
was a tribute paid to his wonderfully picturesque
vocabulary, richest when he was descanting on
the woes he had to endure as a candidate for
medical and scientific honours—whereas he
wanted to be an artist.   He was of angelic temper.

In early September of 1895 three of us,
Gurney Lubbock, McB., and I, took our new
bicycles and started on one of the longest of
our tours, from Dieppe to Nuremberg—nay,
even to Ratisbon.   No contretemps of the road
(and, what with accidents, and the phenomenal
perennial pigheadedness of French railwaymen
about luggage, there were enough of these) ever
produced in McB. anything approaching irrita-
tion : while the courage which enabled him to
seize by its sinewy leg the largest spider I have
ever seen in a derelict bath at Verdun commanded
the deepest respect.   Perhaps, however, the
expeditions I made in his company to Denmark
and Sweden a few years later were the most
blissful of all that I ever had.   They also were
bicycling tours, and on two of the three Will
Stone was the third in company : the last was
after his death, in 1901.   He, son of E. D. Stone
of Eton and brother of E. W. Stone (more nearly
my contemporary), was another ideal companion.
His literary sense was of the finest : a little
memorial volume remains to show what promise
was in him.   There were also, what one asks for

in a travelling companion, affection and humour and a power of simple enjoyment and a willingness to be pleased. Hans Andersen and the old ballads had already prepared me to find in Denmark what I daresay a great many people do not look for there—a land of romance. The first evening we spent there fully answered expectation, as we lay on the edge of the river in the big meadow by Ribe and watched the behaviour of the storks on the housetops over against us, with Ribe cathedral tower in the background, and a most radiant sunset sky. The limit of our journey that time was Wisby in Gothland ; the landing there was marked by our meeting (as per arrangement made earlier at King's) Fred Whitting—waving and trumpeting at us from the quay. We attended a circus at Wisby, and the tan about our feet was full of spiders almost as truculent as that of Verdun.

A monument of this journey and of the peculiar excellence of McB. as a comic artist is extant in a few hands, in the shape of a volume called *The Story of a Troll-hunt*, written and drawn by him. He also began illustrating my *Ghost Stories of an Antiquary ;* the plates he finished are in the first edition : but he died in June 1904, within a year after he had married.

Some memories of Eustace Talbot, whom we lost just a year later, were put into print for his family. Everyone who saw how he was shaping for his profession of doctor was clear that a very distinguished career was assured for him. Everyone who before that saw much of him as an undergraduate would have told you that whether he was going to be distinguished or not he was a great creature and an exceedingly lovable one. Not many people could exhilarate you so certainly : I had to forgive his depredations (and Sir Walter Fletcher's) among the cigars which I kept for the special use of the *Family*, and his (shall I say their ?) sadly unscrupulous behaviour at the game of *Jacobi*. I forgive also, but cannot forget, the shock I suffered when, as I was seated inoffensively in my room, and doubtless engaged in some suggestive and helpful work, the door opened and there entered not only Eustace Talbot but Geoffrey Lyttelton, Neville Talbot, Walter Fletcher, and, I think, George Lyttelton, none of whom appeared to be less than six feet three inches high, and several of them (in the dim light) much larger than that.

Mark Sykes made his appearance in 1897, at Jesus. He was coached for his Little-go by E. G. Swain of King's, and Swain introduced him to me. Not many weeks had passed before he became one of my most constant visitors. On many an evening he would appear at nine and stay till midnight : I might be the only company, but that was no deterrent. Mark would keep me amused—more than amused—hysterical—for the whole three hours. It might be dialogues with

a pessimistic tenant in Holderness, or speeches
of his Palestine dragoman Isa (never repeated
after Isa was dead), or the whole of a melodrama
he had seen lately, in which he acted all the parts
at once with amazing skill. Whatever it was, there
was genius in it. He was quite young, only just
eighteen at this time, but his hopelessly miscellaneous education, which would have killed all
desire or power to learn in most people, had really
suited him in some ways remarkably well, and
given him a much wider outlook than others of
his age have. Yet he was not that detestable
thing, a cosmopolitan : he was very English,
very robust, totally without affectation : keenly
alive to absurdities wherever met : at the same
time profoundly serious about his religion.
The Roman Church could not have had a
faithfuller son.

In the spring of '98, as usual, he was off to the
East. I told him to mind and copy any inscriptions he came across. Now he really did not
know any Greek : yet in the summer he brought
me a note-book with copies of some few Greek
inscriptions, which happened to have been
printed in Waddington and Le Bas : his copies
were better in several places, but he had no notion
of the meaning. I conceived a very high idea
of the confidence that might be put in the work
of a boy who could do this : it showed a great
degree of truthfulness as well as intelligence.
Then he went to the Boer War, and came through

it, and home with a largely augmented repertory
of Yorkshire and Cockney soldiers, angry generals,
and what not ? Then politics, and all the
richness of the House of Commons, Lloyd
George, Ellis Griffiths, Keir Hardie. But I
cannot even catalogue his activities. Public
life never spoilt his simplicity and friendliness :
but it is natural for me to revert oftenest to the
beginnings, and think of the delirious evenings
in which it was perfectly useless to think you
could possibly get anything done, the moment
you saw Mark put a round enquiring face (into
which he would throw the expression of a stage
yokel) round the edge of the door. You had
either to be stern and say you were busy, or else
resign yourself, preferably the latter. Charles
Gatty often came to add more mirth, and also
music : though unnecessarily critical of the
qualities of the piano. As far as I remember
there was only *one* of the pedals that was
seriously out of order, and the proportion of
notes that would not sound was really negligible.

Harold Lubbock I first met in company with
Arthur Benson, who had been his tutor at Eton,
when Arthur was living at the Old Granary by
Silver Street bridge. That will have been in
1904. Just as in all these other cases, it is difficult
to remember how soon he chose to pay me visits
uninvited : but the process may have been
quickened up by the fact that we had a great

friend in common away from Cambridge, in the shape of Owen Hugh Smith.

Harold was a youth of great independence of mind and no slave to custom, and no respecter of persons. He had a delicious gift of humour, into which some vinegar might be infused. To me he was considerate, affectionate, impudent : but what is the use of writing down adjectives, however right they may be ? This at least must be added, that, like his brother Eric (whom I do but name here, with reverence—others have written of him), he was of unwavering dutifulness and undaunted courage, and made the sacrifice of his life without hesitation. A stray shell killed him on the 4th of April, 1918 : he had been married in June of 1914.

With him, and the beloved Geoffrey Tatham, who passed out but a few days before him, I made one of those spring expeditions to France which I am becoming afraid to mention again : with Harold, more than one. The camera, we know, has its place : it may serve to remind us of many beautiful and inspiring scenes : but those who have reached what they are pleased to call years of discretion do not ask it to remind them of times when with bare feet they were wading across a flooded piece of road and very vainly attempting to avoid the sharper stones : nor of those moments when, after a temperate repast, they were taking a short and well-earned nap on some grassy bank. Yet such were the moments which Harold seemed to take a particular pleasure in commemorating. I preserve the results as an effective antidote to complacency.

All these were of the number whose mere presence gives a certainty of delight. In my gratitude to them and for them I am not to make any distinctions or comparisons. That I have had and still have many friends of whom I could write in the same strain they know, and I am thankful.

XXII

As to my official employments in King's. For some years after 1888 I held the Divinity Lectureship. I do not think that lecturing was ever my *forte*, as it was certainly never one of my pleasures. In 1889 I added to it the office of Dean, which I held till 1900, when I accepted under severe pressure the Tutorship and held that for two years. Only my admirable successor W. H. Macaulay could tell how many loose threads I left for him to join up ; and he is too forgiving to wish to do so. The Deanship, then, was the most enduring of these offices. I had two colleagues : first Dr. A. H. Cooke, who was my senior, then Dr. A. E. Brooke, who was my junior ; but the titles Senior and Junior Dean are not statutable in King's. Chapel services, the care of the Choir-School, and the ordinary discipline of the College are the concerns of the Deans. So I have here an opportunity of saying something about that which surely must always be the central feature of King's, the Chapel and its services.

First, of the fabric. During my time two very important pieces of work were undertaken. One was the releading of fourteen of the windows, to which nothing had been done since 1765—seven on the north side, six on the south, and the east window. The remainder had been dealt with—and pretty severely—by the glass painter Hedgeland, in 1845-49. Mr. C. E. Kempe was put in charge of this very interesting work : it lasted from 1893 to 1906, one window being treated every year, and the same skilled workman, Mr. Horace Jackson, saw it all through. A scaffold with many floors was put up, from which every part of the window could be got at with complete ease. This was moved from window to window as required. Great was the excitement, when a fresh window was thus made accessible, of going all over it, settling what mistakes must be rectified, what glaring modern patches should be taken out and replaced by neutral-tinted glass, and what ancient patches were worth removing and preserving ; for it had been the habit of the eighteenth century repairers to stop up holes with pieces of old glass that they had by them, and some of these were of considerable beauty and interest. I collected a large stock of them, had them leaded together, and kept them till some opportunity of using them to good purpose should occur. That has now happened. Mr. E. Milner White, now Dean, has been principally instrumental in getting them arranged and placed in the windows of the side chapels on the south which lead up to the College War Memorial Chapel, the eastern-

most on that side. And with extraordinary
enterprise he has secured—for the most part in
Cambridge itself—some remarkably fine old
glass of the right period for the building, which
fills several windows in the same side chapels.

Curious discoveries sometimes rewarded one's
scrutiny of the windows, as they successively
came to be treated. In one case we found a
date : elsewhere a fragment of what must have
been quite a large composition, representing
gold and silver coins of Charles I, with the
date 1634, suggesting an activity in glass-making
in Laudian times which has not left much trace ;
or again, found that on the Tables of the Law
in another picture there was an inscription in
Flemish ; or that the original painters of some
of the inscribed scrolls had been so lazy or
stupid as to duplicate them, or put them in the
wrong window.

The other work was the remodelling of the
furniture of the eastern bay. As I first knew it,
it was lined with woodwork in the Gothic
manner, designed by James Essex about 1775,
which was very notable work of its time ; the
chief defect being that all the detail was modelled
on the *stone* decorations of the Chapel. A fund
started by generous Kingsmen for the replacing
of this by something more suitable had long been
in existence. It was now to bear fruit. When
you have to take counsel with a body of forty-six
persons on a question of taste, unanimity is not

easily secured. Everybody has an opinion : they are " not experts," they " know nothing about it," they " only know what they like." I should be loth to pass through the many stages of committees, reports, discussions, again. At one time we thought of decorating the eastern bay with hangings. Two panels were made ; then that project was dropped. The hangings are now to be seen on the western wall of the Hall. We ended up with a Renaissance stone altar by Garner and Renaissance wood-work by Messrs. Blow and Billerey. But the Essex woodwork has all been preserved : a considerable portion of the panelling now lines the walls of the passage at the west end of the Hall.

Taste, by the way, was also brought to bear on the internal decoration of the Hall. This is a Gothic building of 1823, by Wilkins. It has an elaborate plaster roof copied from the timber roof of Crosby Hall. This roof had never been touched since the day it was put up. It was whitish and extremely dirty. It positively had to be cleaned, which would mean a scaffolding : ought we not to take the opportunity of applying some colour to it ? We all said Yes to this : the question was, what colour ? A proposal to decorate it . in what the young men described as " polygamy " found some favour. (The word actually used was polychromy, but the young are culpably inaccurate.) I said No :

I preferred something soberer—I might have said, chaster. Let us pretend that the roof really is of timber, and colour it brown, with touches of gold. This is what was eventually done. So few of my designs in the domain of art have met with acceptance that I feel compelled to record this success.

I have said, and I now repeat, that the Chapel services had been marvellously improved in the ten years before I came up. In 1871 the same body of Lay Clerks served Trinity and King's, and the King's Choristers were boys from the town who lived at their homes, and, like the Winchester queristers, waited (extremely ill, I am told) in Hall. In 1871 Trinity abrogated the very slovenly arrangement about the Lay Clerks, and we followed suit. In 1876 a Boarding School for Choristers was started on a small scale, and very soon took its present form, that of a capacious house built by the College in the West Road, the Choristerships being now opened for competition to boys from all parts of the country. In these reforms, which ended by making the King's Chapel services famous wherever Church music is loved, the great agents were Augustus and Willy Leigh and Nixon. But I do not know, I do not think, that they would have succeeded as they did, but for the co-operation of an all-important official who was appointed in that same year 1876 and is still —I write on the verge of the year 1926—to the profound thankfulness of Kingsmen, where he was. In 1755 Dr. Randall became organist of King's, in 1800 Dr. Pratt, in 1855 Mr. Amps, in 1876 Dr. A. H. Mann. Is that a noteworthy record, or is it not? It is not more noteworthy than the record of excellence established and maintained in our music since 1876.

It was part of my duty as Dean to assist at the Choristership trials. I do not think that such a thing has been described in print. Let me try my hand on this new subject. On the day appointed, knots of parents accompanying small boys would be seen in the court at an early hour. At 11 o'clock the boys would be sifted out and set down to a simple examination in Hall, presided over by the Master of the Choristers. From this they were summoned out by a senior chorister (patronizing and amused) half a dozen at a time, and ushered into the Combination Room, there to find about six enormous men in black gowns, and a table with Prayer-books set out upon it. Why they did not at once burst into tears and request to be led from the apartment I cannot imagine ; but only a few of them did. There were the Provost, the Vice-Provost, two Deans, perhaps two chaplains, and the organist. The competitors were put into chairs round the table, and each was requested, in turn, to read a few verses of a Psalm—generally the 49th. This was to test their powers in reading, and to see whether any of them had an accent of more than ordinary poignancy. There was every degree of attainment, of course, from the infant who traced the lines with his forefinger and audibly spelt the words out, to the one who shot ahead and had finished ten verses before you could tell him to stop. There was also the shy one who subsided into tears : he had to be beckoned to your side, and there in the intervals of sobs he whispered into your ear, " Wherefore should I fear in the days of wickedness," and the rest. The reading trial over, we adjourned to the practice-room, and here Dr. Mann took command. Relays of boys stood in a row by the piano and sang scales and were dodged about the keyboard. Amazing, the optimism of parents, who would cheerfully send in a boy whose best effort was like that of a duck with an influenza cold. However, no one was allowed by Dr. Mann to think he had given less than complete satisfaction. After the most terrific performance, the Doctor, with a bright smile irradiating his face, invariably said, " Thank you very much ; that's very nice indeed." (Then to us)—" Do you wish to hear any more, Provost ? " (No, thank you.) " Any more, Vice-Provost ? " (No, I think not.) " Any more, gentlemen ? Very well, my boy, you can run away now." Not until the door had closed behind them did he give way to the mirth that possessed him. The least competent boys were generally those who brought a roll of music under their arms, and came prepared to give us " O for the wings of a Dove " with the full strength of the instrument, but were warded off, firmly, yet with no wounding of suscepti-bilities. In the end, five or six select boys would be taken into Chapel, and, to a somewhat larger audience, would each sing a hymn they knew. This would compensate for all the weariness of the morning : the child had ceased by that time to be nervous—" had strangely forgotten to weep "—and one was in no hurry to cut off the lovely sound.

As a rule the Choir School did not depend on the Fellows for its amusement ; but once a year, in the Long Vacation, an athletic contest took place, which I am given to understand was regarded as far more important than any match with another School or Choir. The Fellows brought an Eleven against the School. Much might be written of those great days. For the majority of the visiting team it was the one day's cricket of the year. Occasionally a player would take a mean advantage of this and become so intoxicated with success that he resisted messages sent from the Pavilion and had to be shame-lessly run out. Such a manœuvre, however, had to be very adroitly managed. The Chor-isters were very much on the *qui vive*, and bitterly resented any appearance of being leniently treated. I received a very sharp admonition myself from the Master, Mr. Benham, when, after exerting every nerve and muscle in the effort to reach and hold a catch, I had finally dropped it. "The boys don't care about being *allowed* to win the match, you know." Everyone, of course, was put on to bowl : I seem to have seen longer overs on that field than on any other, reaching as many as fourteen deliveries of the ball. My own performances are still a source of pride to me. Left-handed lobs, some of which took the form of full pitches, while others barely reached the objective wicket (for it is by no means easy, you must know, to get the range and also induce the ball to leave your hand at exactly the right moment), these were the articles served out ; nor without effect. They so bewildered the recipients that I have quite often taken three of the best wickets of the side in a couple of overs : *and have then been taken off*, I hope not from motives of jealousy.

Augustus Leigh used to tell of a match won on that field before a ball was bowled to the winning side. It was thus. The King's boys played the Trinity boys, the match to be decided on one innings. Trinity won the toss and were all out for o ; King's went in, and Trinity opened with a No-ball. Q.E.D. It is my only cricket story, and even if it is a chestnut it has to find a place. Besides, is it not a little one ?

The Chapel services went on over Christmas Day, so the Choristers must not be neglected in the matter of festivities. I think, indeed, they had quite as many parties as they would have had at home. The entertainments took many forms, centering, of course, round a copious Tea.

And now I approach, with diffidence, a more serious subject. It is difficult for any artist to trace the predisposing causes of his greatest efforts : whether it was the atmosphere of the time, whether the persuasion of friends, or what subtler cause was at work, who shall tell ? It is certain that in two successive years (1895 and '96) single performances of plays written by myself during the preceding week took place on the stage of the A.D.C. (kindly lent by J.)—plays which I believe to have anticipated with singular accuracy the effects of those realistic dramas of a later day which are known as *Grand Guignol*. The audience was so strictly limited that their names were printed on the play-bills : the Choristers formed the majority.

It is in fulfilment of a promise (or threat) made earlier in these pages that I proceed to say a little more of my two tragedies (do we call them a dilogy ? Better not, perhaps). Both were on well-known themes : that of the first was the Western tale of *Bluebeard*, that of the second the Eastern romance of *Ali Baba*. They were— they are—in prose, interspersed with lyrics written by the Rev. E. G. Swain and set to music by Dr. Mann. In both cases the time of the action was transferred from an unknown past to the present day, and the scene to Cambridge. A further touch of actuality was imparted by the introduction of personages well known at King's, including Mr. Nixon in the character of Senior Robber among the Forty Thieves : for the Band was composed of the Fellows of the College, who had been driven by Agricultural Depression to adopt this new line of life. The cave was, in fact, in their garden in the Backs.

There is no doubt that terror if not pity was stirred by these performances. One of the then Choristers has since told me that it was long before he recovered from the shock of seeing and hearing Gurney Lubbock (the last but one of many Ladies Bluebeard) forced, hoarsely screaming, into a sausage machine, whence, as the handle was feverishly turned by Bluebeard, long strings of sausages, represented by air balloons of many colours, issued and were gathered up in his apron by the grim massive L. F. Giblin—then an International Rugby player, now a ruler of Tasmania—the housekeeper of Henry Blew Beard. Nor was an irony more than Sophoclean (if I may say so) wanting. It was upon one of these same sausages that (as the tragedy moved on to its close) Bluebeard's foot slipped as he chased Fatima round the stage, brandishing a horribly serrated knife ; and thus it came about that he fell against the old tower from which Sister

Anne (Will Stone) was beckoning the rescuers
on, and, with the tower, she (whose weight was
computed for dramatic purposes at twenty
stone) fell upon Bluebeard and crushed the life
out of him.

In the other play it is possible that the climax
was reached in the slaughter of Cassim. That
was, indeed, accomplished within the cave, but
the utterances of the victim and the executioners
left no doubt as to the methods that were being
employed. The remains were neatly packed
in the suitcase which Cassim had brought to
take away his loot in : Ali Baba found it lying
inside the cave door when he came anxiously
seeking his brother-in-law, and took it home.
The opening of this suitcase I take to have been
another of the memorable moments of the
play. . . . .

I hope that in dwelling so long on work which
happens to be my own I am actuated less by the
pride of the author than by an interest in the
evolution of the drama. There is a great
deal of talk now about Pirandello and Tchehov
and what not : I sometimes think it would do
impresarios no harm if they occasionally looked
a little nearer home.

I should dearly like to recapture the spirit of
some of the pre-War Christmases at King's.
The College was emptied of undergraduates,
saving the Choral Scholars, and if we had been
left to ourselves I do not know that we should

have been more than gravely cheerful. But a faithful party would assemble from Eton, my tutor, Ainger, Ramsay, being the most constant elements, to which a varying fringe was added of friends who for once in a way were not keeping a Christmas at home. It would be Christmas Eve : we of the College surpliced ourselves and repaired to Chapel. Choir and ante-chapel were full, and dark. Just before the clock struck five the boys would issue from their vestry on the north side, the men from the Hacombleyn chantry on the south ; last, the officers came from the Brassie chantry, and, led by Walter Littlechild with his silver verge, proceeded westwards and took their stand near the south door. A faint musical hum was heard, of the choir taking up the note, and then—it seemed to give the very spirit of Christmas—the boys broke quite softly into " Once in Royal David's city," and began moving eastward. With the second verse the men joined in. I declare I do not know what has moved me more than this did, and still does when I recall it. The service went on. The Lectionary gave us the 60th of Isaiah, " Arise, shine, for thy light is come," for the First Lesson ; the 15th of Revelation, with the sea of glass and the harpers, for the Second. The anthem would be " Prepare ye the way " (*Wise*) or " In dulci jubilo "—" There the bells are ringing *In Regis curia*"—and at the end of all there would be two Carols ; these for choice, " Like

silver lamps in a distant shrine " and " A Virgin
unspotted " (yes, with Stainer's unregenerate
harmonies).

Probably there was no orgy with the Choristers
that evening : it had taken place before. Anyhow,
at the set hour we met to dine in Hall, everybody
at the High Table, where, besides the normal
drinks, hot spiced beer was pressed on us, in our
largest silver tankard. The Choral Scholars
might slip out towards the end of dinner, and
suddenly we would hear from the western
gallery their quartet, led, we will say, by the
delicious alto of Horace Wyndham Thomas.
" When the crimson sun was set " is music that
lingers in memory still. He came to us from
Monmouth School, and had no previous associations with Cambridge. Within a few days
everyone was calling him Tommy : he played
Rugby for the University, acted in the Marlowe
Society's plays, was not particularly clever,
elicited affection everywhere, and was killed in the
War. For us and for him it was a very happy
Providence that brought him to King's.

Combination Room followed Hall, where it was
important to see that certain members of the
party did not get hold of the snuff-box (if
they did, conversation was rendered impossible
by the crashing sneezes which occurred every five
seconds) : where also Dr. Walter Fletcher,
coming from Trinity, was apt to produce some
horrid contrivance (reminding one of the book

called " A Hundred Ways of Making Uncle
Jump ") to the terror and confusion of staid,
white-haired men. And then, perhaps, a game
of cards : then possibly an adjournment of a few
of the company, and a ghost story composed at
fever heat, but not always able to ward off sleep
from some listener's eye (this rankles a little still) :
and so to bed with what appetites we might.

All very pedestrian and Anglican and Victorian
and everything else that it ought not to be : but
I should like well enough to have it over again.

XXIII

I HARK back yet again and take up the subject of socialities, as represented by clubs and societies.

I did not as an undergraduate belong to the Union, and, so far as I know, I was never present at a debate there in my life. If membership could have resulted in giving me any confidence as a speaker, why, then, I missed much-needed opportunities of improvement. From any other point of view I don't feel much regret. The elections to office used periodically to cause excitement in Union circles : some men were quite wrapped up in Union politics. If they enjoyed it, so much the better : to me the game of political intrigue on a small (or large) scale has never been interesting. However, I did come into the Union sphere for a short time in 1885-6, when Leo Maxse persuaded me to accept office as librarian. The large library of the Society was to be transferred to new rooms : I was no use as a librarian in the large sense, but I did superintend the transfer and re-arrangement with a good deal of interest. Then I was away from Cambridge and gave up the office as soon as I could.

To the Committee of the Pitt I was elected as the King's representative in my second or third year. Not very long after, the President, Mr Gunton of Magdalene, gave up, and I succeeded him and remained in office a good many years. We had our breezes in early days : I shan't blow on the old coals, though indeed I doubt if anybody now living could stir them into flame. Ten years or so of Presidency were very pleasant : one met, periodically, some of the leading undergraduates from several Colleges, for the President gave a yearly (or was it a terminal ?) dinner, and members of the Committee in rotation a terminal one. The elections, which took place at these dinners, were sometimes amusing, sometimes embarrassing : as when a candidate was rejected and his backers were sufficiently numerous to blackball everybody else. At first there would be a pretence of ignoring what was afoot ; when that ceased to be possible, all faces would set into resentful gloom, as the box went round the table, and round again. The President, who, as far as I remember, did not vote, used at length to suggest a compromise : if he chose the right moment—then indeed the water began to quench the fire, the fire began to burn the stick, and everything else followed in due course, so that the little pig jumped over the stile and we got home that night. Otherwise "we did not part as I could wish, but bearing malice in our arts."

Of more domestic societies the Chitchat was the most respectable and long-lived. It had been

founded about 1860 by members chiefly of
Trinity Hall and Sidney. In course of time
membership gravitated to Trinity and King's :
those two Colleges furnished practically all the
Society in my time. It met on Saturdays at
10 p.m.: the host read a paper, and either there
was a discussion or there was not. Concomitants
were coffee, dishes of whales (anchovy toast) in
the fender, a cup, and snuff passed round before
the paper, of which everyone had to partake.
The box was presented by F. W. Maitland : *I
have it still.* The fact is that the Society is
dead : like many others of its kind, it was
killed by a secretary of unbusiness-like habits,
whose name I could but will not divulge. The
possession of the books had insensibly devolved
upon me as the oldest and most constantly
resident member. When it became quite clear
to me that there would be no revival, I consulted
a few other old members, and presented the
books to the University Library. But I could not
think that the Library wanted a small snuff-box ;
so I kept it.

The Chitchat was supposed to be—when I
first knew it—the favourite recruiting ground for
a more ancient and exalted society known as the
Apostles. Its proper name was the Cambridge
Conversazione Club, and it dates back to the
days of Tennyson and Hallam. The members
of it would never allow that it was known by
any other name, and constantly denied that they

were Apostles. In my time the belief was that when you were elected to the Chitchat, an Apostle would invite you to take a walk with him one afternoon, and would then probe your capacity for philosophic speculation. You might be found wanting : if the experiment was ever tried on me, as to which I am in doubt, that certainly was the result. Or you might be elected : in which case you must of necessity resign the Chitchat, for the Apostles met on the same day at the same hour. In this manner we of the Chitchat lost H. B. Smith, Tatham, and I don't know how many others in my day : but the evil was of older growth, for among the rules of the Chitchat was one specially aimed at the Apostles, to the effect that No member should ever join (or that Every Member should undertake not to join) any Society that held its meetings on Saturday nights. Need I say that it had not the slightest practical effect?

The only actual members of the Chitchat were undergraduates. With your B.A. you became honorary, but might still attend meetings, and this was very regularly done by a sprinkling of seniors, William Cunningham, Tilley, Waldstein, Dimsdale, myself. E. F. Benson has described a memorable and explosive scene at such a meeting : not, I am bound to say, with entire accuracy—but perhaps it would be pedantic to ask for that

More domestic still, and less longaevous—yes,

and of less exalted purpose—was the T.A.F.
(Twice A Fortnight) Jem Stephen had so
christened the party of his friends which used
to sup together on Sundays when he was an
undergraduate. It was at his suggestion that the
name and custom were revived by perhaps a
dozen of us in 1886. The arrangement lasted
till about 1892. We drew in our chairs to a
piece of dinner in some room of convenient size
in King's or Trinity, and we solaced ourselves
afterwards, it might be with music, it might
be with conversation. There was no Book of
Rules and no written constitution : only few
if any resident guests were allowed. Elections
were by common consent. If it had a short life,
the Society had a merry one. One or two
annual dinners took place in town in the Christmas holidays, to which everyone invited a guest
or two. A regular programme was drawn out
on these occasions, to which all members of
necessity contributed. At one of these, the
pièce de résistance was a tragedy based on the
Westcott-Nixon saga. I am sorry to say that
in a fit of temper which he would have been
among the first, if not the very first, to regret,
Dr. Westcott had actually killed a defenceless
old applewoman. But, owing to a train of
mischances, the knife with which the rash act had
been committed was found in the possession
of Nixon (I must own that this seems to point
to some connivance at least on Dr. Westcott's

part). The upshot was the arrest of Nixon as he was delivering one of his Gresham lectures on Rhetoric, and his trial and execution, the latter carried out with great neatness and dispatch by Marwood (Francis Ford), who arrived very smartly dressed and bringing the rope in a small new handbag. Dr. Westcott was a deeply affected spectator of the misfortunes of his friend, but, doubtless for his own wise reasons, abstained from intervening in any way to prevent the catastrophe.

The last Society which needs to be commemorated here is the Family. The origins of this are obscure, for the early records were destroyed in some fire. It is, however, constantly affirmed that it was in the beginning a Jacobite Club, and that the Family (whose health is its one toast) is the Stuart family. Jacobite or not, it lives on as a dining club consisting of twelve residents (of years of discretion) and meeting fortnightly on Fridays during term at the abodes of its several members in an order settled annually at the end of the Easter Term. From the day I joined it—somewhere in the nineties—till I left Cambridge and automatically ceased to be a member, its meetings were things to look forward to. At that time, in addition to the ordinary members, there was one who was honorary, A. G. Day, once tutor of Caius, then Rector of Great Melton, near Norwich. The resident members when I joined included J. W.

Clark, Ben Latham, Fred Whitting, J. Prior, Newton, Hughes, Jebb, J. J. Thomson, J. N. Langley, J. D. Duff, Neil of Pembroke. Walter Durnford, Arthur Benson, Shipley, Newall, Geoffrey Tatham, R. V. Laurence, Walter Fletcher, were among later accessions.

There was little formality : whist was played after dinner—Day, who was rather deaf, carrying on a moaning soliloquy of " Crazy ! Crazy ! Seventy years have I played, and never a trump in my hand ! " (a palpable exaggeration.) Day was critical of the menu. He always preserved it carefully and took it home : as early as opportunity offered he went in to Norwich and discussed it in detail with his old friend Canon Heaviside, pointing out where, in his opinion, mistakes had been made ; doubtless in terms such as these, which I have heard him use : " Two white meats together." " Needn't have had that second sweet, Whitting : nobody touched it." As he walked back one night with Whitting and me from dining in Magdalene with Professor Newton, I recall his saying in a loud crying voice, " The soup wasn't what you expect from a College kitchen, and I *hate* mackerel ! " His own dinner, an extra one, was given in the Christmas vacation at Caius. For this he always provided a swan from the swannery at Great St. Helen's, Norwich, where they practise fatting these birds for the table (and, in my judgment, don't turn out a very interesting

article after all).   On this occasion his invitation
to Jebb was always written in Greek verse, and
Jebb regularly replied in the same medium :
probably with more mastery than Day, though
Day was a good scholar of an old-fashioned type.

Prior, so long tutor of Trinity, contributed
vastly to the mirth of our meetings.   Latham
used to tell how a rumour once reached Cambridge that Prior had been captured by brigands
in Greece and was held to ransom for £3,000, and
how he, Latham, had set on foot a subscription
among members of the Family to raise this sum
and save their valued friend : " but," he said,
" after several weeks I could only see my way to
seven and sixpence."   " And that was *promised*,"
Prior said ruefully.   Prior's own style of humour
is very hard to set down.   There were romances
about a visit to Constantinople in the company
of Lightfoot, and how Prior had either restrained
Lightfoot from climbing the walls of the Sultan's
palace at night, or had rescued him when he was
caught in the act.   But most of it is evanescent.
Sallies were begun with the repetition of the
same phrase a great many times—" No, but I
want to know I want to know I want to know "—
which is not in the least funny in itself, but somehow served to pave the way.   I do remember one
simple thing that made me laugh.   He had been
telling me how he was cooped up in Venice for
some time by floods.   " Dear me ! did you manage
to get anything to eat ? "   " I don't know I

don't know I don't know. I know a great
many things got *me* to eat," says Prior in a
lamentable voice, peering over his spectacles at
the menu, and bursting into cries of laughter at
the end. So you see it was not *recherché* wit :
but then I am afraid I like the simple jokes best
and we have high authority for saying that it is
no bad thing to laugh easily.

XXIV

From 1893 to 1908 I was Director of the Fitz-william Museum : beyond the acquisition of a few very good MSS (and cataloguing the MS collection) I don't think I can claim to have rendered any lasting service in that capacity. When (as soon as I could after becoming Provost of King's) I surrendered the direction to Mr. S. C. Cockerell, then indeed a bright new era dawned upon it, and there cannot be many similar institutions which can chronicle larger expansions and greater accessions than have accrued to the Fitzwilliam in his time and by his means.

The staff of the Museum in my day were all in their various degrees most admirable helpers, taking a pride in the institution and in their work : but I must single out H. A. Chapman, the Principal Assistant, who died at the beginning of 1910, for a very particular tribute of gratitude. I could fill a long paragraph with dwelling on his excellences : but I know that panegyric, unless it can be made pictorial, is very dull reading, and I have not the skill to colour the picture aright.

At that time, and for long after, the Museum of Classical Archaeology in Little St. Mary's Lane

was under the Director's control. I mention
it because the Senior Assistant there, Mr.
Cowman (respectability incarnate), furnished me
with a phrase I want to preserve. A subordinate
had been detected in liquor : in fact, the habit
was growing on the poor man. Now the
Museum is or was principally a collection of
casts of classical sculpture. The room which you
enter first—that where the attendant was stationed—contains the earliest products. Mr. Cowman, anxious to find excuses for his colleague,
said to me, " Yes, Sir, I know it's very serious :
but there is allowances to be made for him : you
see, Sir, he sets in the archaic period." (You
catch the connexion of ideas ? A long contem-
plation of the Apollo of Tenea and the sepul-
chral reliefs of Sparta forces the maddened
victim to seek solace in the Bowl. Perhaps this
is in people's minds when they talk of the elevating influence of Hellenic art.) Admirable Mr.
Cowman ! he had been one of Rattee & Kett's
very best workmen, and knew all about furniture, and secured for me for the sum of £4 a chair
from Mildenhall of which the present value may
roughly be described as above rubies.

How many public functions, how many
academic controversies, have I not passed
sub silentio ? Women's Degrees, Greek in the
Little-go, proposed alterations in the University
Library ? Are they not, with the resultant
discussions in the Senate House, written in the

pages of the *University Reporter*? and did I
not, on leaving Cambridge, joyfully commit to
the destructor all the back files of that journal
which I possessed? One phrase that occurred in
a discussion I will preserve. Dr. Mayo, speaking
of two proposals that were before the House,
said that they were mutually suicidal.

How many people, eminent in University
life, and full of kindness to me, have I quite
consciously refrained from describing and prais-
ing! Why is there nothing about Sir Richard
Jebb, Dr. Butler, Lord Acton, Sir Robert
Ball, Dr. Hort, and a score of others? Why do
not I dwell on the real nobility and saintliness of
Westcott? on Swete and Gwatkin? on Maitland,
Jenkinson, Herbert Ryle, Adolphus Ward, George
Humphry, Newton, Hughes, Stanford?

Partly because others have done all this
worthily, but very largely because the reader knows
perfectly well that a dreadful satiety, ending in
an unreasoning dislike for the subjects, arises
from a perusal of a List of Benefactors. This
book is not that, nor does it emulate Burgon's
Twelve Good Men, from the reading of which I
always come away with an admiration that is
combined with most unregenerate sentiments.
Nor yet is it a collection of obituary notices,
though it comes, I see, perilously near that in
several spots, in spite of my protestations on
page 64. My object has been to present as
often as I could the very ordinary human aspect,

and not to leave out the comic side where I happen to have seen it. To follow that line in some cases would be to hurt someone's feelings, inevitably. In other cases I have not retained the image in my own mind with sufficient sharpness to transmit it to others.

XXV

In May 1905 I was elected Provost of King's, and moved into the Lodge early in 1906. This necessitated a change of habits. Without having a very clear-cut conception of the duties of a Head of a House, I was at least certain that he ought to be easily accessible to all estates in the College, and I am glad to say that this conception found a response, so that on most evenings I could still look forward to casual visits, which were facilitated by the substitution of a handle for a keyhole on the front door.

The pleasures of the uppermost rooms at feasts and the chief seats in the synagogues were for me considerably discounted by the having to occupy also the uppermost room at College meetings. Though the inexperienced Provost was nobly supported and ably prompted by skilled assessors, Vice-Provost, Bursars, and Tutor, the fact is not to be disguised that on the morning of such a gathering, especially that of the last Tuesday in November, called the Annual Congregation, he—I—woke up with a load of depression on the chest which only lifted when we dispersed, after sitting perhaps from 11 to 7 o'clock. Nay, even a Committee meeting was enough to damp my spirits in anticipation : it damps them now. I have never had the least satisfaction in what is called " dealing with men," or in the " sense of power." My highest hopes when I take the chair are that I shall not make any dreadful mistake and that no personal question will arise. The consciousness that you are directing the destinies of a great institution, which should always be present to your mind, is, except on rare occasions, too apt to disappear, veiled in a mist of smallnesses, financial, agricultural, educational—lecture fees, pigsties, servants' wages, plans for the new bathroom at the Manor Farm. Well for you if these things, in all of which you may be able to summon up, at least for the moment, a genuine interest, constitute the whole of the day's business, and if nothing under the head of " Appointments, Re-appointments and Stipends " involves delicate questions of the efficiency of a lecturer, or aught else that brings the personal question on the tapis. Those are the moments that bead the brow with perspiration and shorten and darken the life of him who has, if he can, to guide and control the discussion and cannot possibly avoid listening to it. These are sad but sincere confessions.

Two functions of a more welcome kind now fell to me : one, the visiting of College estates, going circuit, as we called it, with C. E. Grant as Bursar. This meant perambulating Devon, Dorset, Wilts, Hants, and sometimes Norfolk and Suffolk. It took place in alternate years. I don't think it yielded me any picturesque stories, but it meant wholesome walks over farms, and drives—in a wagonette—along the Chalke Valley, or in the New Forest country, and Sundays at Sherborne, or Exeter, or, above all, Sarum. The other was the official connection with Eton, of which the Provost of King's is *ex-officio* Senior Fellow. If Henry VIII had had any of the instincts of a gentleman, we should no doubt have held our meetings in the Leper Hospital of St. James's (where his palace now stands) ; but, as is known, " Henricus Octavus took away from us more than he gave us " (it is a hexameter, and you have to say Henrĭcus), and we did in fact meet in one of the most gloomy rooms in the Westminster Palace Hotel, hung with portraits of Freemasons, and little consonant with our dignity. I used to find myself sitting next to Sir Henry Roscoe, for whom I soon began to feel a cordial affection. He was a tremendous figure of a man, with a glorious Northern accent : rather deaf, which led him to impart very damaging criticisms to me in what he fondly supposed to be a whisper. " He doosn't know what he's talkin' about." " Ssh ! Ssh ! he'll hear you, Sir Henry." " No, he won't hear me : I say he doosn't know what he's talkin' about, and it's a very serious matter. (*Louder*)—Mr. Provost, I want to know——" But Provost Hornby could also assume a judicious deafness, and would say, " Yes, I think we'd better be gettin' on now ! " Whereat Sir Henry would subside into a rumbling murmur, and expound his point to me during the luncheon interval. There was a bigness about him in all ways, and an overflowing kindliness which I learnt to value very much. The other wonderful old man on our body at that time was Lord Halsbury, whose vigour was a constant marvel. Usually he left our meetings early : a myth arose that it was in order to secure the best of the umbrellas : it was a dreadful imputation to cast upon a Lord Chancellor, but it is unde-niable that anxious glances were cast towards the umbrella-stand, and sometimes a Fellow would rise and pursue Lord Halsbury from the room, with a hasty apology to the Provost, and return bearing what he *said* was his own umbrella.

The years went on : College business fulfilled its round. University business increased : one joined more Syndicates and Special Boards ; the most interesting were the Library and the Press Syndicates, of both of which I became chairman at dates I have not recorded. France was still being regularly visited at Easter time, and in August A. B. Ramsay, Anstey Guthrie and I were the nucleus of bicycling parties, usually again in France, but sometimes in Scandinavia or Germany or Austria. Catalogues of MSS, books for the Roxburghe Club (to which I was elected in 1909), with occasionally a lighter volume, were being turned out at short intervals. In 1910 I became a member of a Royal Commission on Public Records. But for the War a great deal of good might have resulted from the investigations of this body, which took one to all sorts of curious places, including the Victoria Tower in Westminster Palace, where all the original Acts of Parliament are stored, and the basements of Government offices, and the triforium of the Abbey, yes, and the Metropolitan Water Board at Surbiton. To me this Commission brought a private joy in the acquaintance with Dr. Henry Owen, the Pembrokeshire antiquary. The first bond of union was that we both smoked *pipes* after lunch. Before very long he had engaged me to come to his delightful house at Poyston, near Haverford-west, which I first saw in June 1913, and after that almost every year till his death in 1919. The later visits I generally paid with A. B. Ramsay, towards the end of August. Dr. Owen would be at the front door to welcome us : the first question always was, " How long are you going to stay ? " Some polite hesitation was expressed. " No, I want to know. *I* don't care how long it is. I want to know when to order the fly." When that was settled, he said, " What do you want to drink after dinner ? " a question similarly fenced with, and also settled with satisfactory results. The days were tranquil : a toddle to the post-box in the lane about half-past twelve: perhaps a bicycle ride to St. David's (that was laborious) or Slebech, or a walk to the rath : hours in the excellent library : a concert from the rooks at sundown, an evening of cards and tobacco. These are the sober pleasures of a person who begins to confess that his body at least is elderly. It was delightful too to see how Henry Owen was thought of in the region : at the station the flyman would say, " Going to Dr. Owen's, Sir ? Ah, you'll be all right there, indeed." You felt that a halo hung about you as you walked the lanes, because you had been seen in his pew at Rudbaxton church.

Among the occasional duties of a Head, one is to act as a delegate of the University to other Universities which are celebrating centenaries or are starting on their career. Twice in 1911 I had this honour, at St. Andrews' and at Rennes in Brittany. *Il y a des longueurs*, alike for hosts and guests. The thing must be done, but the sigh of relief that follows comes from the heart. Of course you see some beautiful things, you *may* hear some fine oratory, and you meet some interesting people ; nor do you always refrain from smiles, as at the sight of that great old hero Sir James Murray of the *Dictionary*, wearing eleven doctors' hoods at the same time with childlike pleasure. Nor from groans, as when you rise at 6 a.m. and put on evening clothes forthwith, according to the vicious and foolish

Continental custom, and at once feel as if you
had been up all night ; or when, having repaired
to a solemn banquet at 7, you leave it on the
stroke of midnight, when the Gaekwar of
Baroda has just risen to propose the thirtieth
toast. There are limits. But on neither occasion was there any limit to the kindness of my
particular hosts, Dr. Playfair at St. Andrews' and
Professor Feuillerat at Rennes.

XXVI

In October 1913 Stuart Donaldson, Master of Magdalene, who had been Vice-Chancellor for a year, was forbidden by his doctor to continue the work for a second year : I was next on the roster, and had expected to assume office in 1914 : now I had to take it at ten days' notice. Providential, because to begin in the first October of the War would have been far harder. As it was, I had a year of normal academic life in which to learn the routine. It is one long chairmanship. Persons have been found who said they rather liked it. Of course, it is the Permanent Officials who make the work possible for a neophyte. Dr. Keynes, Registrary, and Secretary to the Council of the Senate, spent every Saturday morning with me coaching me for the horrors of the Monday meeting : the Secretaries of the various Syndicates and Boards pushed me through the steps of the quadrille : the Esquire Bedells and the Marshal told me what I must do and say in the Senate House (but did not tell me what to say when a Bishop taking a D.D. made a now obsolete Declaration in Latin and said *persĕvērăbo*). By hook or by crook, but more by the kind activities of these persons, and the goodwill of those over whose deliberations I presided, I was helped through the year : the Easter term ended with the giving of somewhat less than a thousand degrees and the signing of about an acre of cheques. At Midsummer I retired into Norfolk with a bicycle and explored some of the best churches with Walter Fletcher and Richard Lyttelton, saw a fine Eton win at Lord's, rambled over part of Essex with the Commission on Historical Monuments ; and then came August 4th, 1914.

On the Sunday I was in a country church in Kent, praying for peace. On the Monday I went back to Cambridge, and then began the long succession of consultations in which emergency legislation was devised, the resources of the University placed at the disposal of authority, measures settled with the Town as to action in case of hostile landings : later, when Liège and Louvain fell, the invitation to Belgian professors and students was issued. A kind of branch War Office for the issue of commissions was set up in the Hall of Corpus, where Walter Durnford and many another gave all-day attendances. A hospital was fitted up in the cloister of Nevile's Court at Trinity, then transferred to the King's and Clare field, and enormously expanded. The buildings still cumber what was the fairest of all the College playing fields. Then came camps on Mid-

summer Common, and regimental messes established in College Halls—welcome indeed they
were.

It is hard to judge, but I think that, among
those who saw no active service, they whose
life was bound up with a University or a great
school had some of the most poignant experiences of the War, in the constant partings with
the young. The two first to whom I said good-
bye at the Lodge door were of those who did not
return.

But I am in no mood to recall every stage
of those troublous times, which, as the months
passed, did not relax their grip, though abnor-
mal conditions came to seem normal. The
young men in King's grew fewer : we had no
cadets to replace them, for our only possible
building was filled with the nurses of the
hospital. Emptier and emptier grew the
courts, slower and duller the pulse of life :
and .be it remembered, among the many false
prophecies of the time, that it was commonly
predicted that none of those who had served
would care to return and finish their course,
and that the Universities would be empty
for years to come. Exactly the contrary was
the case.

Typical of the background of one's thoughts
during those years were the evenings when an
air-raid threatened, and the lights went down,
and you sat wondering what the next hour

would bring forth. Typical also the summer
days when, having bicycled out a few miles into
the country, you lay on the grass by the
roadside and listened to the throb of the guns in
France.

XXVII

In the early summer of 1918, Dr. Warre, who had for some time been in failing health, asked the Visitor (the Bishop of Lincoln) to accept his resignation of the Provostship of Eton. He had been anxious to do this at an earlier date, but the Fellows had dissuaded him, in the hope that strength might yet come back to him. The date at which resignation should take effect was fixed for Michaelmas Day. In July I received through the Prime Minister the intimation of the gracious pleasure of the Crown that I should succeed Dr. Warre as Provost of Eton. It is curious, but true, that no translation of a Provost from either of Henry VI's colleges to the other had ever taken place before. Of the early Provosts of Eton, Waynflete and Aldrich had been Head Masters, of eleven later ones (beginning with Bland in 1732), eight. Four Head Masters at least had become Provosts of King's ; and, under the old dispensation, you would naturally find that several of the Provosts of Eton had been fellows of King's in their time. But the precise thing that happened in my case was new.

Thirty-six years had I spent in King's : only

twenty elsewhere. But if I was to leave it for any other place, Eton was the place for which I would least unwillingly leave it ; and if one time for leaving it could be easier than another, it was the moment when its life was at the lowest ebb, and there was least to be done there.

I most thankfully accepted the gracious offer that had been made. On the morning of Michaelmas Day, which was a Sunday, I knocked at the entrance door of School Yard, and, entering, was received by the Fellows, the Head Master, Lower Master and Staff, and the assembled School. I must say that when I so entered a strong feeling possessed me that I had come home again. That feeling, natural in itself, was intensified by the fact that among the Masters were many friends of long standing, and, above all, that my Tutor was one of those who were gathered in School Yard to greet me.

One cannot chronicle with the same freedom of comment the events of the seven years that have passed since then. We have had our troubles—largely money troubles. The School is full, but College is poor. We have had our controversies : questions of Taste have stirred passions to a fever-heat at times : our losses, too, not to be lightly numbered or weighed. Warre, Ainger, Rawlins, de Havilland, H. B. Smith, John Rawlinson—the two last-named among the wisest of all counsellors of the College —that is a list very full of meaning to Etonians,

And now, alas! the name of Walter Durnford has to be added to it.

On the other hand, Eton is always putting out new growths. Under the Lower Master, A. B. Ramsay, who has now transferred the sphere of his beneficent rule from Eton to Magdalene, the Choir of Lower Chapel has grown into a valued institution. The interior of that building, too, has taken on a new aspect conformable with the beauty of the services. That is the work of the War Memorial Council. When the four tapestries of the history of St. George are all in place, that interior will be hard to match. Then, where ugly sheds and gasometers stood, the gifts of benefactors such as Mr. Prideaux, Miss Edmonds and Mr. Askew, have, under the Head Master's skilful guidance, reared Palaces of Art and rows of covered fives courts in comely red brick. A new voice has been given to School Hall in Mr. Luxmoore's and Mr. Askew's organ, and new light and heat to College Chapel, again by Mr. Askew's hand.

To live in the midst of Eton certainly makes on the whole for cheerfulness, especially to one who, while he moves about among 1,100 boys, few of whom appear to be suffering from depression of spirits, is at the same time not burdened with the correction of their excesses. I have quoted Oscar Browning's complaint that schoolboys always laugh at you. All I can say is, let them. It is no unpleasant reflection that you may be affording innocent enjoyment to the young by the observation or recollection of your little peculiarities. . . . At the same time, what they can possibly find to be amused at is, I own, a puzzle to me. Forty years back, now, I grant you, there *were* some very odd people about the place.

I pay my tribute to the humour of boys, which excels in simplicity and directness. It is difficult, however, to approve it unreservedly when it takes a practical form. On the last day of one summer half, say in 1881, I went to say good-bye to Miss Jane Evans, and waited some few minutes in her parlour ; when she came down she was rather flustered. " What do you think ? " she said ; " the boys' maid called me into one of my Lower boys' rooms just now, and I found that one of his friends had been spreading the whole of the inside of his portmanteau with raspberry jam." Can you conceive anything more devilish ? I think the retribution was that the boys exchanged portmanteaus : I hope so.

Not the humour alone of boys do I praise. It is hazardous to go further, for no sooner do you begin to generalize about their virtues than you are staggered by the news of some totally unexpected misdemeanour. They are not to be calculated upon. They are always breaking out in fresh places. Yet . . yet . . I am persuaded that the race is a good race. Superficially observed, it is better than the race I knew ; or, if not better, certainly nicer. I do not want to over-state, but I am tempted to give them a high mark for courtesy, considerateness, intelligence, good-will, and, when they reach positions of influence, trustworthiness and real desire to do the right thing.

I know that such observations as I am able to make must be heavily discounted. An experienced tutor can tell you, and make no mistake, that Mr. Plausible, Mr. Facing-both-ways, Mr. Pick-thank are the real names of those you have been calling Faithful, Greatheart, Valiant-for-truth. I know that the faces shown to contemporaries are often very different from those I see. But I am not disillusioned.

Visitors come to Eton and go away calling it a Paradise for boys. In the main they are right, and in the main I am right when I say that though no boy is going to pass through Eton without woes—very often of his own making—he is not going to find any other five or six years in his life which will pile up more memories that he is glad to keep. Nor, I think I must add, while he is here, is there much more interesting company than his to be found, if he is at all a fair specimen of the Eton boy.

EPILOGUE

LOOKING back over the pages of my manuscript, I am tempted to fear that there may be in them too much apology for the levity of the contents. Too much, because perhaps readers will find them heavy : too much, because one object has actually been to suggest that a bookish, unadventurous life can be quite a cheerful one : and that the perception of the ridiculous is not the perquisite of the young alone.

But when I come to write the last pages of a book of reminiscences, I feel that levity is no longer in place. I allow myself to dwell on the thought of the real greatness, the augustness, of the ancient institutions in which I have lived : to which I have owed the means of gaining knowledge, the noble environment that can exalt the spirit, the supplying of temporal needs, and almost every single one of the friendships that give light to life : have owed all this and more for nigh on fifty years.

In the forecourt of each of the Colleges stands the figure of the man who made all this possible for me and for thousands of others. In their Halls and galleries are the pictures of those who made them famous, governed them wisely, added to their power for good, re-shaped their old laws to meet the needs of the time. Of the Founder we may have but a dim conception : we can at least be sure that his spirit was so righteous and gentle that he would have rejoiced in the felicity of his chosen.

Of our heroes, benefactors and counsellors we have ourselves known some, and realize our debt to them : for the rest, the whole tale of what they have done is so varied that surely everyone can find something in it to give him a lead. Even the man whose greatest achievement has been to revise College Statutes has probably by that ungrateful labour made the path to learning easier of access, and may have become the collateral ancestor of some great service to the world. At least it is sure that from all these, the Founder, and the builders of Eton and King's, we have received more benefits visible and invisible than we can possibly repay. Some time or other we beneficiaries shall be asking ourselves, as I do now, whether we have been contented to lie down under the debt, or have made a real effort to acknowledge it. A question not lightly to be answered.

Education, religion, learning, and research are defined in the Statutes of King's as the causes which the College is to foster. I hope that it does, and I hope that Eton, whose Statutes contain no such definition, is no less a friend to the same causes. Centres of light let both of them be, and let both be dear through life to their sons, as mothers of the happiness of youth.

LET Thy blessing, O Lord, be upon the Colleges
of Thy servant King Henry the Sixth : and as
Thou hast appointed unto them diversities of
gifts, grant them also the same spirit : that they
may together serve Thee to the welfare of this
realm, the benefit of all men, and Thy honour
and glory : through Jesus Christ our Lord.

Amen.

PRINTED BY THE WHITEFRIARS PRESS, LTD., LONDON AND TONBRIDGE.

www.ingramcontent.com/pod-product-compliance
Ingram Content Group UK Ltd.
Pitfield, Milton Keynes, MK11 3LW, UK
UKHW010347140625
459647UK00010B/879